Absolute Surrender
Andrew Murray

BOOKS BY ANDREW MURRAY
FROM BETHANY HOUSE PUBLISHERS
With Updated Language

Abiding in Christ
Absolute Surrender
The Andrew Murray Daily Reader
The Blood of Christ
The Fullness of the Spirit
‒ *Humility*
The Indwelling Spirit
‒ *A Life of Obedience*
Living a Prayerful Life
The Ministry of Intercessory Prayer
The Path to Holiness
Teach Me to Pray

Absolute Surrender
Andrew Murray

BETHANYHOUSE
Minneapolis, Minnesota

Library of Congress Cataloging-in-Publication Data

Murray, Andrew, 1828–1917
    (Believer's absolute surrender)
    Absolute surrender / by Andrew Murray
        p. cm.
Originally published: The believer's absolute surrender. Minneapolis, Minn. : Bethany House Publishers, ©1985, in series: Andrew Murray Christian maturity library.
    ISBN 0-7642-2815-3
    1. Christian life—Reformed authors. I. Title.
    BV4501.3.M877   2003
    248.4—dc21   2003006508

ANDREW MURRAY was born in South Africa in 1828. After receiving his education in Scotland and Holland, he returned to Africa and spent many years as a missionary pastor. He and his wife, Emma, raised eight children. He is best known for his many devotional books, including some of the most enduring classics of Christian literature.

Contents

Introduction

By way of introduction, it should be noted that the following chapters were originally sermons delivered at the Keswick Convention. For those readers who have never attended such a convention, I will clarify the reason why the messages were first preached and are now published.

The best explanation is found in citing the origins of the Keswick Convention. Canon Battersby had for more than twenty years been an earnest evangelical minister, known and recognized as a godly man. But that godliness bore the common mark of today's believer: a sense of one's life not being pleasing to God. The painful defeat in the battle with sin and the frequent loss of the joy of God's presence makes the perfect peace and abiding fellowship of which the Word speaks impossible. Before the great Oxford Convention, Battersby had been deeply stirred by the news that some there would testify to victory over sin and continuous walking in the light as the rule of their Christian experience. He saw that there were promises in God's Word to warrant this, but he did not know how to receive them. At the convention, he heard a message on faith as *resting on Christ's Word*, and saw that by faith he could claim and receive the power of Christ to do in him what he had before thought impossible. The Spirit of God opened his understanding to see this and confirmed this great fact in him, so that he was ready to testify to what God had done for him.

The Keswick Convention had its origin in the desire to give this testimony in wider circles. Battersby spoke with others of the old life they had lived, of the new life and joy God had given, and of the simple way in which through faith they had found the passage from the one to the other. The blessing that followed was far-reaching. Many who were longing for a holy life found the help they needed. In the power and joy of the Holy Spirit, an atmosphere was created of which the presence is felt even as I write. The intensely personal call to confession and surrender of what was wrong in the past, the joyous testimony of what Christ made possible, and the uncomplicated appeal to come and by a single act of faith prove God's faithfulness and power, brought a message and a blessing that many had never heard or dreamed possible.

These chapters will attempt to illustrate the three major goals that marked these conventions.

Their first goal was to uncover the lie that a carnal Christian life is all that is possible. Nothing does more harm in the body of Christ than the underlying thought that obedience is impossible. Until believers see the error of this and honestly view their life of continual failure as sinful and inexcusable, no amount of preaching will help. To walk after the flesh, continually yielding to self-will, is contrary to what God requires of us.

The second goal of this teaching is to make clear that God has made provision in Christ, our Savior from sin, and by the Holy Spirit dwelling in us, by which the life of victory and rest and fellowship can be maintained. Christ in His saving power can be real and present with us moment by moment. It is only as we see plainly in God's Word this life prepared for us that we can be encouraged to hope for it.

The third goal was to show that the transition from the old life of stumbling and broken fellowship can be made in a moment by one decisive step. This is possible because it is nothing more than an act of faith in Christ, trusting Him to work in us what we have failed to do ourselves.

I ask that my readers regard this book as a very simple personal appeal. Ask God to show you whether you are walking in the path of absolute surrender and close fellowship to which you are called. If you read my book as a scholar, merely to gather more truths into notebooks, or as one simply desiring to be edified, you will very likely be disappointed. But if you read it as one who desires deliverance from sin, you will very likely be blessed.

With the humble prayer that God might by His Spirit bless the written page as it has pleased Him to bless the spoken word when we were gathered in His presence, I commit this book and its readers to His holy care.

Andrew Murray

— *Chapter 1* —

Be Filled With the Spirit

These well-known words concerning the Holy Spirit are found in Acts 2:4: "They were all filled with the Holy Spirit." And in Ephesians 5:18: "Be filled with the Spirit." The one text is a narrative; it tells us what actually happened. The other is a command; it tells us what we should be. If there is any doubt about its being a command, we find it linked to another in the first part of the passage in Ephesians: "Do not get drunk on wine, which leads to debauchery. Instead . . ."

If I were to ask you if you tried to obey the command not to be drunk with wine, you would no doubt answer, "Of course, as a believer, I obey that command." But what of the other: "Be filled with the Spirit"? Have you obeyed it as well? Does your life manifest the presence of the Holy Spirit? If not, my next question is, Are you willing to take the command to heart and say, "By God's help I will obey. I will not rest until I am filled with the Spirit"?

From the very beginning, limit yourself to the question of whether or not you will hear and obey the simple command in God's Word. Put away for the moment varying notions and conceptions about the filling of the Holy Spirit. We want to close in on the one object we are aiming at and the message we believe

God has for every believer: "My child, I want you to be filled with the Spirit." May your answer be: "Father, I want it too. I yield myself to obey your Word. Fill me with your Spirit now."

My first clarification regarding being filled with the Spirit is that it does *not* mean a state of high emotion. Nor does it mean absolute perfection or a level at which there can be no more growth. Being filled with the Spirit is simply this: The whole personality is yielded to His power. When the soul is yielded to the Holy Spirit, God himself will fill it.

Now the question comes, "What is needed in order to be filled with the Spirit?" To find the answer we must allow God to search our lives. We might ask ourselves, "Am I in the condition in which God can fill me with His Spirit?" Some of you may be able to honestly answer, "Thank God, I am ready." If you can say this, you may realize that you have been kept back from this full blessing by lack of knowledge, prejudice, unbelief, or a wrong idea about what being filled with the Spirit is.

Let us look at the way Christ prepared His disciples for the Day of Pentecost. Jesus had His disciples for three years in a type of "baptismal class." This was their time of training and preparation—much as a missionary might train candidates for baptism in a country where Christ has not before been preached. The coming of the Holy Spirit at Pentecost upon the church was not magic, neither was it an arbitrary event. The disciples were prepared for it. John the Baptist told them what was to come. He not only preached the Lamb of God who was to shed His blood but he also told them that He on whom he (John) saw the Holy Spirit descend would baptize with the Holy Spirit.

Let us look further at what was involved in the training of

those disciples. How were they prepared for the baptism of the Holy Spirit?

First of all, remember that these were men who had forsaken all to follow Jesus. Jesus asked the fishermen to leave their nets; He asked another to leave his tax collecting. Peter said, "We have left everything to follow you!"—their homes, their extended families, their work, their good name. They were mocked and laughed at for leaving all to follow Jesus. People called them *the disciples of Jesus,* which was considered a mockery. When Jesus was despised and hated, they were hated too. They identified themselves with Him; they utterly yielded themselves to do His will, to go wherever he commanded.

For us too, this is the first step in the way to the baptism of the Holy Spirit: We must forsake all to follow Christ.

I am not speaking here about forsaking *sin*—that you do when you first come to Christ and are converted. But there is something more for us as His children. Many believers think that when they receive Jesus, He saves them and then helps them in times of trouble. Then they all but deny Him as their Master! They think they have a right to have their own will and their own way in a thousand things. They say what they want to say, do whatever they like to do, and use their property and possessions as they wish; they are their own masters and would never dream of saying, "Jesus, I forsake all to follow you."

And yet this is the command of Christ. He is the Lord of all we have and are. We cannot have Him in us and with us unless we yield everything to Him. Jesus' words have not changed: "Forsake all and follow me."

Recently I was at Johannesburg and heard a simple story of what is being done there in God's kingdom. At a gathering of believers to testify of what God had done for them, a woman stood and told how some six months before she had received such a wonderful blessing through the infilling of God's Spirit. At a consecration meeting, the minister had asked who of them were ready to yield themselves entirely to Jesus. He asked them to prepare themselves to answer by supposing He were to ask them to go to China, or to give up their spouse or their children. And she said earnestly, "I *did* want to say I would give up everything for Jesus, but I could not. When he asked those who were willing to stand, I stood and said, 'Yes, I will give up everything.' Yet I felt as if I could not give up my husband and children. I went home, but I could not sleep; I could not rest, for there was the struggle: Must I give up *everything*? I *wanted* to do it for the sake of Jesus. It was past midnight, and I said, 'Lord, yes, for you, *everything!*' And the joy and the power of the Spirit flowed into my heart." Her minister testified of her too, that now she walked in the joy of the Lord.

Perhaps you have never made the same commitment or never thought it was necessary. Are you willing to say, "O Lord, let me be filled with the Holy Spirit; I surrender anything and everything to you"?

Each of us must examine our own heart. Some have never thought it a necessity to do so. Some have never understood what it meant when Jesus said, "If anyone comes to me and does not hate his father and mother, his wife and children, his brothers and sisters—yes, even his own life—he cannot be my disciple" (Luke 14:26). Or when He said, "And everyone who has left houses or brothers or sisters or father or mother or children or fields for my sake will receive a hundred times as much and will inherit eternal life." Our love for God must be greater than all of these. Surely our lack of victory over sin and the reason the Holy Spirit does not fill us is because we have not forsaken all to follow Christ.

A second thought to consider is that these were not only men who had forsaken all to follow Jesus, but they were *intensely attached to Him*. Jesus had said, "If you love me, obey me; and I will ask the Father and he will give you another Comforter" (John 14:15–16 TLB). And they *did* love Him. They had seen Him crucified, but their hearts could not be separated from Him. They had no hope or joy or comfort on earth without Him; and this is what is so often lacking among us. We trust Jesus and His work on Calvary; we trust Him as our only Savior; that is sufficient to bring us salvation. But there is the relationship of an intense, close, personal attachment to Jesus and fellowship with Him every day—the relationship that means that Jesus, the unseen One, shall be my Friend and Guide and Keeper at all times, my Leader and Master whom I obey. But it seems there are few who understand these thoughts.

This is one of the strong elements of the Keswick Convention teaching. A few years ago a young missionary came out to South Africa and spoke of the blessing she had received at Keswick. She told me that as a child she had loved the Lord Jesus and had been educated in a circle of godly friends and a godly home, but what a difference it had made when she found what it is to receive the filling of the Holy Spirit. I said to her, "You have from your childhood lived in a bright, godly atmosphere; what do you think is the difference between the life you lived then and the life you have entered into?" Her quick answer was simple: "It is the personal fellowship of Jesus."

Believer, this is the beginning of the deeper blessing. Some people would forsake everything for the sake of their religion.

Even for a false religion multitudes have given up all. Some would forsake all for their church. Some would give up all for the sake of their family or friends. But that is not what is asked of us. We must forsake all for the sake of Jesus, let Him come into our life and take possession of our heart. Is your life one of tender personal attachment to Jesus and of joy in Him? I am not asking if your love is perfect. I am asking if you can say honestly, "It is what I am striving after, what I have yielded myself to, what I long for above everything. Jesus Christ must have all of me every day and all the day."

A third thought is this: These disciples were *men who had been led to despair of themselves*. At the beginning of their three years of instruction they had to give up all they possessed; but it was only at the end of that time that they began to give up themselves. They had given up their nets, their homes, their friends, and that was right; but throughout the three years how strong "self" was! How often Jesus spoke to them about humility! But they could not understand Him. Time after time there was contention among them as to who should be chief. The night before the Crucifixion they were still arguing over it. They had not given up self. It was obvious to all how little they lived in the Spirit of Jesus!

But Christ taught them and trained them. He revealed to them time after time what the sin of pride is and what the glory of humility is so that when He died on the cross, they died too. Think of Peter, the impetuous disciple, having denied his Lord. Don't you think that in all the sorrow of those three days, from the Crucifixion to the Resurrection, the deepest and the bitterest was his shame at the thought of how he had treated his Lord? At the supper table how self-confident he had been! "Even if all fall away on account of you, I never will" (Matthew 26:33). But Jesus took him with Him in His death and the grave, and then Peter knew that there was in him, indeed, no good thing. He had learned to despair of himself.

Some of you may say, "I think I have given up all for Jesus— my property, my home, my friends, my position; and I think I do love Him, but I still have not received the blessing. Friend, are you willing that God, with His searchlight, would uncover in you how much there is of self-will and self-trust? Will He not point out your judgment of people, how you speak what you wish and what you think and have not yet learned the humility and tenderness and gentleness that Jesus taught? That is *self*. You work for Him. You try to do good, but all the time it is really your own working. You are doing the work, and you look to God to help and bless. But it is not enough. God must bring each one of us to the place of death with Him.

Do you know what the death of Jesus meant? Jesus said to His Father, in effect, "Here is my life, which has been precious to me. I have not yielded to sin. I have given you all my life while on earth; now I yield it to you in death." He gave up His spirit saying, "Into your hands I commit my spirit." Because He gave up His life so entirely, and passed through the thick darkness of death and the grave, God raised Him up into a new life and new glory. It was His death that was the secret of the Resurrection. If you want to be filled with the Spirit and the risen life of Christ, you must first die to self. The apostles were men who had been brought to a place of utter self-despair. They had lost all, and were ready to receive all from God.

The apostles were *men who had accepted the promise of the Spirit from Jesus by faith.* On the night before the Crucifixion, Christ had spoken to them about the Holy Spirit more than once, and when He was ready to ascend into heaven, He said again, "In a few days you will be baptized with the Holy Spirit" (Acts 1:5). If you had asked those disciples, "What does that mean?" I am sure they could not have told you. They had no concept of what would come. But they took the word of Jesus, and if they had any occasion to discuss the subject during those ten days, I am sure they said something like "If while He was on earth He did such marvelous things for us, now that He is in glory will He not do things infinitely more wonderful?" And they waited for that.

You also must accept this promise by faith and say, "The promise of the filling of the Holy Spirit is for *me*. I accept it from the hand of Jesus." You may not understand it; you may not feel as you would like to feel; you may imagine you are only weak and sinful and far from Jesus; but you may say—and you have a right to say, "The promise is for *me*." Are you ready to do so? Are you ready by faith to trust the promise, and the Word, and Jesus' love for you?

I am sure there are believers who are struggling to find out where they are lacking, even those who have yielded themselves fully to Jesus, who do love Him, and who have sought to humble themselves in any way that they can. But the problem may be that they simply have not learned to say, "He has promised, and He will do it."

For your encouragement, I would add that when you get a promise from God it is worth as much as its fulfillment. A promise brings you into direct contact with God. Honor Him by trusting the promise and obeying Him, and if there is any preparation that you still need, God knows about it; and if there is anything that is yet to be opened up to you, He will do it if you count on

Him to do it. Trust the promise and say, "This fullness of the Holy Spirit is for me."

Finally, *on the strength of the promise, the disciples waited in united prayer.* That is what we must do—wait on God in prayer. They waited, they prayed with one accord; prayer and supplication was offered, mingled with praise. They expected God to do something. It cannot be stressed enough—the importance of expecting God to act. I know believers—I have found it true in my own experience—who read, meditate, desire, claim, reach out to take, and yet what they seek eludes their grasp. It is because they do not wait for God to give it.

Do not look alone to a teaching or to what you think you understand with the idea of receiving a blessing from it. *Look to God alone. Let your expectation be from Him.* It is not enough to believe. I find that many people mistake their personal faith for the blessing that faith is intended to bring. By faith I am to "inherit the promises." Believe and trust God; then look to Him to give the blessing. Be filled with the Holy Spirit.

Chapter 2

The Joy of Being Filled With the Spirit

My purpose is to try to set before you the joy of a life filled with the Holy Spirit. We clarified the way in which the disciples were led to receive the blessing; now let us look at their joy in being filled with the Spirit. It may please God to make our desire so strong, and to make us see so clearly, *This is what I need, I cannot live any longer without it,* that He may bring us to receive more than we ever expected. He is our God, who is willing and able to do far above all we could ask or think.

The clearest illustration of the joy of being filled with the Spirit is seen in the wonderful change that Pentecost brought to the lives of the disciples. It is one of the most wonderful object lessons in all of Scripture—the Twelve under Christ's training for three years, and yet remaining, apparently, at some distance from the life they were meant to live; and then all at once, by the blessed incoming of the Holy Spirit, being made just what God wanted them to be.

Look first at *the change that Pentecost brought into their relationship with Jesus.* During His earthly ministry, of course, Jesus could not live in the Twelve. He was outside them, separated—very near, very loving; and yet, if I may say so with deep reverence, Christ's teaching to them was lacking. Until the Holy Spirit came. Christ tried to teach them humility: He said, "Learn from me, for I am gentle and humble in heart" (Matthew 11:29) and "Whoever humbles himself will be exalted" (Matthew 23:12). Yet right up to the end they were still contending among themselves which of them was the greatest.

Christ did not conquer their pride. This was not due to a lack of divine teaching. The reason was because of the fact that Christ was outside them and could not yet dwell in their hearts to empower them. The time had not yet come. They had the almighty Redeemer alongside them but not in them. This teaches us that no outward instruction, even from Christ himself, or His words in Scripture, can bring us the full blessing—until the Holy Spirit works it *in* us.

But what a change took place on the Day of Pentecost! He had told them that on that day they would know He was in them. Christ in us—not in the sense that we are in a particular room. We can leave a room, even come and go freely. But the Lord Jesus came to be literally—I say it with reverence—part of us, to fill our hearts and thoughts and affections; and what Peter and James and John had when they had Christ alongside them, you and I have in a much larger measure, if we have the living Christ within us.

Isn't that what your heart longs for? I have thought and thought of Jesus in Bethlehem, of Jesus on Calvary, of Jesus upon the throne, and I have worshiped and loved and rejoiced exceedingly in Him; but all the time I wanted something better, something deeper, and something nearer. The answer is to have the living Jesus within. That is what the Holy Spirit will give you, and that is why we plead with you: Will you not yield yourself to receive this blessing—to be filled with the Spirit—that the blessed Jesus may be able to take possession of you? Jesus *within*—the very Jesus who is the Almighty One, who died on the cross and sits upon the throne, condescending to be your life.

That is why the Spirit came. Jesus said, "I have given them the glory that you gave me, that they may be one as we are one: I in them and you in me" (John 17:22–23). And what is the glory of Jesus? His love and His power. The Holy Spirit will reveal Christ in us, so that the wonderful love of Christ shall be a possession and a reality in its divine nearness, and that power of Christ shall have the mastery within us. You know the wonderful prayer in Ephesians 3:14–21, that the Father might strengthen them with might by the Spirit in the inner man, that Christ might dwell in their hearts. The mighty power of the Holy Spirit can do it. The Holy Spirit makes Jesus present within us.

Of course, when Jesus walked with them on earth He was not *always* with them. They could not be with Him every moment. You remember that He sent them across the sea while He stayed on the mountain to pray. You remember that He took three of them with Him up into the mountain, but the others stayed below; and there they had to meet the Pharisees and could not cast out the evil spirit. There were times of separation, and at last there came that terrible death, that awful separation from the world. Yes, Christ was their life—sometimes with Christ, and sometimes not with Him; sometimes near Him, and sometimes the crowd pressing around Him, and they could not get to Him.

But *the presence of Jesus by the Holy Spirit is meant to be unbroken, continual, and forever.* This is surely what our hearts long for. Perhaps you know what it is like to live a week or a month in a joy that makes your heart sing all day. Then the change comes with the cloud and the darkness—and you do not know why it is—sometimes with physical sickness or depression, sometimes with the cares and the difficulties of this life, sometimes with the consciousness of your own failure. Oh, that I could convince every believer! Jesus does love you; He does not wish to be separated from you for a moment. He cannot bear it. We want to believe in that love of Jesus. No mother has delighted more in the baby in her arms than does Christ delight in you. He wants both intimate and unceasing fellowship with you. Receive it, beloved believer, and say, "If it is possible, God helping me, I must have this filling of the Holy Spirit, that I may have Jesus always dwelling in my heart."

Notice too the change Pentecost made in their inner life. Until then their life was full of failure and weakness. I have spoken of their pride. Christ had to reprove them for their pride repeatedly. You know how they longed to be faithful to Him, yet their pride and self-confidence were the cause of continual failure. Peter said, "Even if all fall away on account of you, I never will," and all the others said the same; yet, within a few hours they denied Him— the result of pride and self-confidence. They did not know the evil within them. Jesus had done everything to teach them humility, but He could not change their inner weakness. Peter had said, "Even if I have to die for you, I will never disown you," but at the word of a maidservant he began to swear and to declare that he never knew the Man. *What utter weakness!*

But then came the change of Pentecost! I will not say they had victory over sin, for I do not think it came in that way. The Holy Spirit—the Spirit of God—became their life; they were filled with the might and the power of the living Jesus, the Savior from sin.

You know that the primary work of Jesus is to take away sin. How is this done? Many believers imagine His taking it away on the cross. Others go a step further and say, He takes it away from His throne in heaven; He cleanses me and keeps me. But the truth is: If the light comes in, the darkness is expelled. It is the presence of Jesus, indwelling us by the Holy Spirit, which makes us holy. What a change came over the disciples! Notice how boldly they were able to speak in the presence of those who threatened them with death. "We must obey God rather than men," they said. They were sent to prison and there sang praises to God at midnight. It was a wonderful change the Holy Spirit wrought in their lives!

What does this teach us? We often speak of the self-life and the life of the Holy Spirit. Have you ever said to God—perhaps you have said it often—"Lord, how can I be rid of my self-life?" Has God answered you? Has He reached into the deep place of your heart and brought you to say, "O God, my failure is my own self-confidence, self-will, and self-pleasing"? Self will have its say in everything, and there is no power that can expel it but the power of the presence of Jesus.

Do not get entangled in theological definitions as to how it is all done, how much sin remains or how much is cast out. Be content that though you cannot completely explain and expound it, yet you can believe that the Spirit of holiness is simply the holiness of Jesus in your heart. Filled with the Spirit, you have within you the power of the holiness of God to do the work of sanctification.

Third, *the filling of the Holy Spirit changed the disciples' relationship with one another.* Look at *the love that united them into one body.* Before we mentioned that there was selfishness among them, often a lack of love; but when the Holy Spirit came, not only did He work in each individual, but He molded them into one body. They knew they were the members of the Lord Jesus, and because of their love for each other they did things that were utterly unheard of at that time. Though most of them were strangers, they began to sell their goods and give away their property, and to say they had all things in common. This was the result of the Holy Spirit having come down as the very love of God in heaven to dwell in their hearts.

Perhaps you find that your greatest difficulty in life is your relationship with other believers. Very often people who have to work together differ in temperament and character, and how easily friction comes in! Then there are people who differ in regard to some theological truth or practical way of doing Christ's work, and how they speak or write against each other! So there are divisions in Christ's church on earth. Even among those who profess to love God, and profess holiness and entire consecration, disagreements abound. It is a sad state of affairs. There are so many earnest believers who have so much to say about others! They can point out where I am wrong, and I can point out where they are wrong; but how few there are who though distinctly differing with each other can still say, "Above all our differences there is a unity that we must express; we want continual fellowship in the presence of our Father."

Do you want to have a heart overflowing with love to every believer, even to those outside your own circle? Do you want a heart of love that can set others on fire? Do you want the very love of heaven to flow out from you? Do you want the self-sacrificing love of Jesus to take possession of you, so that you can bear and forbear, so that with the longsuffering and tenderness and gentleness, and the very meekness of Christ, the Lamb of God, you are willing to be the helper and servant of everyone, however unlovable or unlovely? Then you need to be filled with the Spirit. Cry for that, claim that, accept that, rest not until you have it. The Spirit is the Spirit of God's love, the Spirit of the crucified love of Jesus. If we receive the Holy Spirit, the love of God will be shed abroad in our hearts, and God will melt us into one as never before.

And then fourth, *the coming of the Holy Spirit changed their works.* What a difference Pentecost made! And I suppose we all feel—at least many of us feel—that this is one of the important things in connection with speaking about being filled with the Holy Spirit. Many Christian workers thank God for the way He has led them on but still feel that they are lacking something. They lack both the continual joy in speaking about Jesus and the consciousness that God is using them as one of His instruments. Yet that is what God wants each of His servants to have. How many Sunday school teachers and Bible study leaders feel this way: "I am not confident, not equipped, even ignorant, but I know God is using me because I have given myself into His hands, and I have consented to be anything at all for Him."

Would it not be unutterable joy to always work in that spirit of absolute humility and dependence with a childlike trust that God will use you? How are you to get to that place? Look at the apostles; look at the disciples. I read that Jesus sent them out to do three things: to preach the Gospel, to heal the sick, and to cast out demons. When they came back they told about the last two—healing the sick and casting out demons; but I do not hear them tell about conversions. Somehow their preaching of the Gospel was lacking. It was done faithfully but without much results.

But when the Day of Pentecost came, their preaching

changed—not only Peter's—they were all proclaiming the mighty works of God. What a difference! And it went on and on. What boldness they had and what largeness of heart! They went on to Samaria and to Caesarea and then to Antioch, and there they waited upon God; within a very few years the Gospel message had been brought into Europe! It was the power of the Holy Spirit that accomplished this. Here we lack the power for our work, whether in the wider fields of missions or in our own neighborhoods.

I thank God for the interest He is awakening in the church for the lost and the unreached or the least reached, but there is still an area that remains neglected. It is often easier to reach the poor, the needy, the downcast. But the middle class, the upper class—is there power in your Christian walk to take the Gospel to them with boldness? Are not many of you members of churches and congregations where you sit Sunday after Sunday with those around you whom you know are unconverted? Is there not a need for divine wisdom and power to equip us for this work? Do we not need divine light and inspiration? Do we not need power with a new love and boldness to pray and wait and work, and to see that not only those who are in China, in Africa, or in other parts of the world shall have the Gospel, but that the Good News shall be brought to those with whom we are associated every day? We thank God that He has in recent times awakened Christians to work as never before, but it is but a beginning. If believers will spend time with God, wait on Him in prayer, and declare that they are ready to do His work, is not God able to do more than He has already done?

One thing is needed. The Spirit did it all on the Day of Pentecost, and He continues to work. It is the Spirit who gives boldness, wisdom, the message, and the converting power.

I am speaking to every believer who feels the need of power. Is your whole heart ready to say that this is what you want? "I see it. Jesus did not send me into warfare on my own orders; He does not ask me to go and preach and teach in my own strength; Jesus intended that I have the fullness of the Holy Spirit, whether I am at home teaching my children or off on a missions trip. Whether I have a small Sunday school class or a larger class of laypeople, the one thing I need is the power of the Holy Spirit. I need to be filled with the Spirit."

Let me conclude by asking, Are you prepared now to receive this from Jesus? He loves to give it. God delights in nothing so much as to honor His Son, and it is honoring to Jesus when souls are filled with the Holy Spirit, because then He proves what He can do for them. Will we not claim it?

Let me give you four simple steps. Everyone who longs for this blessing must say, first of all, "I *must* be filled." Say it to God from the depths of your heart. "God commands it; I cannot live my life as I should without it."

Secondly, say, "I *may* be filled. It is possible; the promise is for me." Settle it and put away all doubts. The apostles, once so full of pride and self-life, were filled with the Holy Spirit because they took hold of Jesus. Likewise, with all your own pride, sin, and self, if you will but cling to Him, you may be filled.

The third step is to say, "I *would* be filled." To gain the "pearl of great price" you must sell all, give up everything. You are willing, are you not? "Everything, Lord, if I may only have your Spirit. Lord, I would have it from you now."

The final step says, "I *shall* be filled. God longs to give it; I shall have it." Never mind whether it comes as a flood or in deep silence; or whether it does not come now because God is

— *Chapter 3* —

The Carnal and
the Spiritual

Our thoughts in this chapter will center around 1 Corinthians 3:1–4: "And I, brethren, could not speak to you as to spiritual people but as to carnal, as to babes in Christ. I fed you with milk and not with solid food; for until now you were not able to receive it, and even now you are still not able; for you are still carnal. For where there are envy, strife, and divisions among you, are you not carnal and behaving like mere men? For when one says, 'I am of Paul,' and another, 'I am of Apollos,' are you not carnal?" (NKJV). The Apostle begins the chapter by telling the Corinthians that there are two levels of Christian living. Some believers are *carnal* (worldly, in the flesh) and some are *spiritual*. By the discernment of the Holy Spirit, Paul saw that the Corinthians were carnal, and he wanted to tell them so. You will find the word *carnal* four times in these four verses.

Paul felt that all his preaching would be useless if he talked about spiritual things to men who were unspiritual. They were believers, real Christians, babes in Christ; but there was one deadly fault—they were *carnal*. He seems to say: I cannot teach you spiritual truth about the spiritual life; you cannot receive it. It was not because they were stupid. They were very clever and full of knowledge, but unable to understand spiritual teaching. Thus, this simple lesson—all the trouble among believers who sometimes receive a blessing and lose it again is because they are *carnal*; if we want to keep the blessing, we must become *spiritual*. We must choose which level of Christian life we desire—the *carnal* life or the *spiritual*. Choose the *spiritual*, and God will be delighted to give it to you.

To understand this teaching, we must begin by explaining what the carnal state is. I will point out four characteristics.

First, the carnal state is a state of protracted infancy. A long time has passed since you were converted. By this time you should be a young man, but you are still a babe in Christ. "I fed you with milk and not with solid food; for until now you were not able to receive it." You know what a beautiful thing babyhood is. Is there anything more delightful than a six-month-old child: rosy cheeks, smiling face, kicking feet, and grasping little fingers? But suppose I saw the same child six months later, and he was not a bit bigger and not doing anything more than he did at six months. The parents would say, "We are afraid there is something wrong; our child is not growing." If after three years I saw that the baby was still no bigger and was not walking or talking, I would find the parents very sad indeed. They would tell me, "The doctor says our child has a rare disease and cannot grow. It is a wonder he is still alive." Ten years later there is still no growth.

Babyhood at the proper time is the most beautiful thing in the world, but babyhood that continues beyond the first few months is a burden and a sorrow, a sign of disease or disorder. And that was the state of many of the Corinthian believers. They continued as babies.

What are the common characteristics of a baby? He cannot help himself, and he cannot help others. And that is true of the life of many believers. They make their ministers into spiritual nursemaids. It is a serious matter when spiritual babies keep their pastors and layworkers continually occupied with nursing and feeding them, and they never help themselves. They do not know how to feed on Christ's Word; the preacher or teacher must feed them. They do not know what contact with God is; the minister must pray for them. They do not know what it is to live as those who have God to help them; they always want to be nursed and cared for. Is that the reason why *you* go to church—to get your nurses to give you spiritual meat? God be praised for the preaching of the Gospel and for the fellowship of believers. But you know what a baby does. He always occupies someone. You cannot leave him alone. Likewise, there are many spiritual infants whom ministers are always attending to. Instead of these believers allowing themselves to be trained up to know their God and be strong, they are held back in a protracted infancy. They cannot help themselves and therefore cannot help others. Is not this what we read of in Hebrews 5:11–6:3? We find there the very same condition: those who had been so long converted and should have been teachers needed themselves to be taught the first principles of Christianity. These are people who always want *to be helped* instead of *being a help* to others.

For a young Christian, a spiritual baby of three months old, to be carnal and not to know how to have victory over sin is, as Paul said, a thing not to be wondered at. But when a man continues year after year in the same state of always being defeated by sin, there is something radically wrong. Nothing can keep a child in protracted infancy except a disease or disorder. And if you have to say continually, "I am not spiritual," then begin to say, "O God, I am carnal; I am in a diseased or disordered state, and I want to be helped out of it."

The *second* characteristic of a carnal state is that *sin and failure prove to be the masters*. Sin has the upper hand. What proof does Paul give that those people were carnal? He first charges them and then he asks a question, "For where there are envy, strife, and divisions among you, are you not carnal and behaving like mere men? For when one says, 'I am of Paul,' and another, 'I am of Apollos,' are you not carnal?" Paul in effect asks, "Isn't it obvious? You act like other men; you are not acting like spiritually renewed men who live in the power and love of the Holy Spirit. You know that God is love, that love is the great commandment, that the cross of Christ is nothing but the evidence of God's love, and that the fruit of the Holy Spirit is love." The whole of John's gospel means *love*. But when men give in to their tempers and pride and envying and divisions; when they hear people saying sharp things about one another; when a man cannot open his heart to a brother who has done him wrong and forgive him; when a woman can speak about her neighbor with contempt—all these are the works of the carnal spirit. Every incidence of being unloving is nothing but the *flesh*. The word *carnal* is a form of the Latin word for *flesh*, and being unloving is nothing but the fruit or work of the flesh. The flesh is selfish and proud; therefore, every sin against love is nothing but proof that the person is carnal.

You may say, "I have tried to conquer it, but I cannot."

Of course you cannot bear spiritual fruit while you are in the carnal state. You must have the Holy Spirit in order to love aright.

Then your flesh will be conquered. He will give you the Spirit so that you can walk in love.

This is true not only of the sins against love but all other sins as well. Worldliness, which someone says has "honeycombed the church"; love of money; the pursuit of business (when people sacrifice everything for the increase of wealth); so much of our life seeks after luxury, pleasure, position. What is it all but the flesh? It gratifies the flesh; it is exactly what the world considers desirable and delights in. If you live like the world, it is proof that the spirit of the world is in you. The carnal state is proven by the power of sin.

Someone asked me recently, "What about a lack of love for prayer?" He wanted to know how loving fellowship with God could be attained. I said, "It is impossible until you discover that it comes outside of the carnal state." The flesh cannot delight in God; that is your difficulty. It is meaningless to say or write down a resolution in your journal: "I will pray more." You cannot force it. But let the axe come to the root of the tree; cut down the carnal mind. How can you cut it down? *You* cannot, but let the Holy Spirit come with the condemnation of sin and the cross of Christ, and give the flesh over to death, and the Spirit of God will come in. Then you will learn to love prayer and love God and love your neighbor, and you will be controlled by humility and spiritual-mindedness. The carnal state is the *root* of every sin.

We have come to the third point. If we want to understand the carnal state thoroughly, we must realize that *the carnal state can coexist with great spiritual gifts.*

Remember, there is a great difference between spiritual gifts and spiritual graces, and that is what many people do not understand. Among the Corinthians, for instance, there were many wonderful spiritual gifts. In the first chapter of the first epistle to the Corinthians, Paul says, "I thank my God ... that you were enriched in everything by Him in all utterance and all knowledge." That was something for which to praise God. And in the second epistle he says in effect, "You do not come behind in any gift; see that you have the gift of liberality also." And in the thirteenth chapter of the first epistle he speaks about the gifts of prophecy, and of faith that could remove mountains, and of knowledge as things that they were pressing in on; but he tells them these will not profit them unless they have *love*. They delighted in the gifts, and did not concern themselves with the graces. But Paul shows them a more excellent way—to learn to love and to be humble. Love is the greatest thing of all, for love is Godlike above everything.

This is a very serious reminder that a person may be gifted in prophecy, be a faithful and successful servant in some particular area, and yet by his sharp judgment and pride, may prove that while spiritual gifts are wonderful to have, his spiritual graces are decidedly absent. Take care that Satan does not deceive you with the thought, "But I work for God, and God blesses me, and others look up to me, and I am the means of helping others." Hear me out: Any person who is exercising spiritual gifts, even the most earnest and successful worker, must be brought to his knees before God with the possibility, *Am I, even after all that God's Spirit has worked in me, giving in to the flesh by my lack of humility, or love, or purity, or holiness?* May God search us and try us, for His name's sake.

The fourth point is that *the carnal state renders it impossible for a man to receive spiritual truth.* This is characterized by believers who hunger for the Word, and they listen and even comment,

"What beautiful truths, what clear doctrines, what wonderful expositions of God's Word!" and yet they receive no help from it; or they are helped for two or three weeks, and the blessing passes away. What is the reason? The carnal state is hindering the reception of spiritual truth.

I am afraid that in our churches we often make a tragic mistake. We preach to carnal believers what is only profitable to spiritual believers. The carnal believer may think it all so beautiful and take it into their head and delight in it and even say, "That is marvelous! What a view of the truth that man presents!" And yet their lives remain unchanged even after all the spiritual teaching they get, because they are carnal. The only evidence that you have *received* a teaching is that you are lifted out of the carnal and into the spiritual state. God is willing to make this happen. Let us plead for it and open our hearts to receive it.

And now comes the very important and solemn question: "Is it possible for a man to move out of the carnal and into the spiritual state? And *how* is this possible?" I will answer this and point out the steps that must be taken.

First, the person who seeks the spiritual life must see that it is possible and have faith for it. Some are so full of unbelief that they cannot accept the fact that it is possible to become spiritual.

While talking to a man of deep Christian experience, I said to him, "Tell me about the state of the believers in your community. You have worked among them and know them well." He replied, "I believe the worst thing about them is their *unbelief*." Then he told me about a young man of great promise who was working for Christ. That young man had many gifts, but my friend could not understand why, with all those gifts, he did not see more results. They spent a whole day together trying to find out what it was that was hindering the young man's ministry. Gradually they discovered that the root of the trouble was his *unbelief*. He did not think it possible to live a consecrated life. He was not sure God was ready to give him such a blessing. The next morning they met again to discuss it further and to pray. During their discussion, the young man finally saw what it was to trust God for the power of a life of full surrender and he received the Holy Spirit. Since then he was tenfold more successful in his work.

Try to catch a vision of the spiritual life for yourself. Believe that if you are ready and willing, God will fill you with His Spirit and make you a spiritual person.

As we have said, the Word speaks of two powers of life—the power of the *flesh* and the power of the *Spirit*: the flesh represents our natural life under the power of sin; the Spirit is God's life coming in to take the place of our natural life. What we need to do is yield our whole life over to Jesus, to identify with His death, to become nothing in ourselves, and then to receive the life of Christ and the power of the Spirit to do all and be all for us.

You may be saying, "That is so far beyond me, I can never reach it." No, you cannot reach it in yourself, but God will reach down to you and give it if you truly believe that He is offering it and wants you to have it. God is able and willing to do more for you than you can ask or think.

I believe it is possible for us to live every day led by the Holy Spirit. We read in God's Word that He sheds abroad His love in our hearts by the Holy Spirit. We also read in God's Word that as many as are led by the Spirit, they are the children of God. If we are born again, we are to walk by the Spirit or in the Spirit. Believe that it *is* possible; it is the life God calls us to and that Christ redeemed us for. After He shed His blood, He ascended into heaven to send the Spirit to His people. After He was glorified, His first work was to give the Holy Spirit. When you begin to believe in the power of Christ's blood to cleanse you and in the power of the glorified Christ to give you His Spirit, you have taken the first step in the right direction.

Though you may feel ever so unworthy, hold fast to Jesus. He can and will fill you with the Spirit, for it is He who has commanded you to be filled with the Spirit!

Second, it is not enough that we should have a vision of the spiritual life; it is imperative that we should be fully convinced of our carnality. This is a difficult and serious lesson, but a necessary one. There is a great difference between the sins of the unconverted and the sins of the believer. As an unconverted person, you had to be convicted of sin and make confession of it. But what were you primarily convicted about? Of gross sin; and you were particularly concerned about the guilt and punishment of it. But there was likely very little conviction of inward attitudes, such as pride, criticism of others, selfishness, arrogance. These convictions do not normally come at conversion. And so how are we to get rid of them? After we become Christians, the Holy Spirit convicts us of the carnal, worldly life and its pursuits. Then we begin to mourn over it and become ashamed of it. We cry out like Paul, "What a wretched man I am! Who will rescue me from this body of death?" (Romans 7:24). We begin to seek for help and to ask, "Where am I to find deliverance?" We seek for it in many ways, by struggle and resolve, but we do not find relief until we cast ourselves completely at the feet of Jesus. Do not forget that if you are to become a spiritual person, if you are to be filled with the Holy Spirit, it must come from God. God alone can do it.

How different our living and praying and preaching would be

if the presence of the Holy Spirit, who fills the universe, were revealed to us! To that end, God wants to bring us to a place of utter brokenness. Somebody said to me, "The call to die to self is a dreadful call." Yes, it is dreadful, if you had to do it in your own strength. But remember that God gave Jesus to die for us, and that God wants to join you into Jesus that you may be delivered from the power of the flesh. If the experience brings you to a place of being utterly broken and in despair, it is only that you may learn to trust in God alone. Paul said, "Indeed, in our hearts we felt the sentence of death. But this happened that we might not rely on ourselves but on God, who raises the dead" (2 Corinthians 1:9). That is the place you must come to under conviction of your carnality. You may cry out, "The flesh prevails and triumphs; I cannot conquer it. Have mercy on me, oh, God!" And God *will*. Only be willing to bow before God in conviction and confession.

Third, believe that one can pass from the carnal to the spiritual condition in one moment of time. People want to *grow out* of the carnal and into the spiritual, but it does not work that way. This kind of thinking requires more preaching and teaching. The child I spoke of earlier, though ten years old, remained like a baby of six months; he had a disease or disorder, and needed healing. Only then could growth come. The carnal state is both a state of disease and disorder. The carnal believer is a babe in Christ. He is a child of God, but he cannot grow. How is the healing to come? It must come through God, and God desires to give it at the moment it is sought.

Let me clarify: The one who becomes *a spiritual person* in a moment's time because of his or her full surrender, is not yet *a person of spiritual maturity*. I cannot expect from a young believer who has received the Holy Spirit in His fullness what I can expect from a mature Christian who has been filled with Him for twenty years. There is a great deal of growth and maturity in the spiritual life. But what I speak of when I speak of *one step* is this: You can change your place, and instead of standing in the *carnal* life, enter the *spiritual* life in one moment.

Note the reason why the two expressions are used. In the carnal person, there is something of the spiritual nature; but things get their names from their most prominent element. Something may be used for two or three purposes, but it will probably get its name from that which is the most prominent. It may have several characteristics, but the name will be given according to that which is the most striking. So Paul says, in other words, to the Corinthians, "I could not address you as spiritual but as worldly—mere infants in Christ . . . for you were not yet ready for it. Indeed, you are still not ready. You are still worldly. For since there is jealousy and quarreling among you, are you not worldly?" (1 Corinthians 3:1–3).

The spiritual person is not one who has reached final perfection; there is still abundant room for growth. But if you look closely, the chief characteristic of that one's nature and conduct is *a person yielded to the Spirit of God.* Though not perfect, he or she is a person who has taken the right position and said, "Lord God, I have given myself to be led by your Spirit. You have received and blessed me, and the Holy Spirit now leads me." It is possible, God helping us, to leave our place on the one side and take it on the other.

You may have heard the story about the sick man, seventy years of age, who was faithfully visited by a minister who talked to him about the blood of Christ. "Oh, yes," responded the man, "I know about the blood of Christ, that it can save us, and about pardon, that if God does not pardon us we cannot enter heaven." Yet the minister saw that the man was under no conviction of sin. Whatever the minister said, the man agreed, but there was no life in it, no conviction. The minister finally despaired one day and prayed, "God, help me to show this man his lost state." Suddenly a thought came to mind. Being near the sea, the floor of the man's room was strewn with sand, and the minister drew a line in it with a stick. On the one side he wrote the words *sin, death, hell*; on the other side, *Christ, life, heaven.* The old man asked, "What are you doing?" The minister answered, "Listen! Do you think one of these letters on the left side could get up and cross the line to the right side?" "Of course not!" was the answer. Then the minister said solemnly, "Neither can a sinner who is on the left side cross over to the right side on his own. The line divides all mankind— the saved on the right, and the unsaved on the left. Only Christ can carry you from the left side over to the right. On what side are you?" There was no answer. The minister prayed with him, and then left, praying that God would convict him of his sin. He went back the next day, and the question was "Well, my friend, on what side are you today?" The man answered with a sigh, "On the wrong side." It was not long before that man welcomed the Gospel and accepted Christ.

I would like to draw a straight line and ask you who believe and confess that God has given you His Spirit and who know the joy of the Holy Spirit, to take your place at the right-hand side. Then I would ask you who have felt that you are still carnal, to come to the left side and say, "God, I must confess that my Christian life is for the most part carnal, under the power of the flesh." Then I would tell you that you cannot save yourselves from the flesh or get rid of it. You must come to Christ afresh; He can lift you over into the new life. You belong to Christ and He belongs to you; what you need is to cast yourselves upon Him and He will reveal the power of His crucifixion in you, to give you victory over the flesh. Cast yourselves, with the confession of sin, and utter helplessness, at the feet of the Lamb of God. He will give you deliverance.

That brings me to my final thought: *We must take the decisive step in faith that Christ is able to keep us.* It is not only a belief; it is not a consecration in any sense of its being in our power; it is not a surrender by the strength of our will. These aspects may be present, but the principal thing is that we look to Christ to keep us today, tomorrow, the next day, and always; we must receive the life of God within us. We want a life that will last not only until another "revival" but until death takes us home. We want, by the grace of God, to experience the almighty indwelling and saving power of Christ and all that God can do for us.

God is waiting; Christ is waiting; the Holy Spirit is waiting. Do you see what has been lacking and why you have been wandering in the wilderness? Do you see the good land, the land of promise, in which God is going to keep and bless you? Remember the story of Caleb and Joshua and the spies. Ten men said in effect, "We can never conquer those people." Two said, "We are able, for God has promised." Step out on the promises of God. Listen to God's Word: "Through Christ Jesus the law of the Spirit of life set me free from the law of sin and death" (Romans 8:2). Take hold of the promises and claim that God will do for you through His Holy Spirit what He has offered to do.

Come to Christ and disregard whether there is any new experience, any feeling, any excitement, any light, or only apparent darkness. Come and stand upon the Word of God. The Father promises His Holy Spirit to every hungry child. Will He not give it to you? How shall He not give the Holy Spirit to those who ask Him? How could He not do it? As surely as Christ was given for you on Calvary, so the Holy Spirit has been given for you and for me. Open your hearts and be filled with the Spirit. Come and trust the blood of Christ for your cleansing; confess your sin, your carnality; then believe in the living Christ to bless you with the presence of His Spirit.

Chapter 4

That God May Be
All in All

*Then the end will come, when he hands over the kingdom to
God the Father after he has destroyed all dominion, authority
and power. For he must reign until he has put all his enemies
under his feet. The last enemy to be destroyed is death. For he
"has put everything under his feet." Now when it says that
everything has been put under him, it is clear that this does not
include God himself, who put everything under Christ.
When he has done this, then the Son himself will be
made subject to him who put everything under him,
so that God may be all in all.*

1 Corinthians 15:24–28

What mystery there is in this section of Scripture! We speak of the
two great acts of humility on the part of the Lord Jesus: His
descending from the throne in heaven and becoming a man upon
earth, a servant among men; and His descent through the cross,
into the grave, and the depth of humiliation under the curse of
sin. But another mystery is spoken of here: The time is coming

when the Son of Man will be subjected to the Father, and shall give the kingdom into the Father's hands, and "God will be all in all"! It is hard to grasp this; it passes our human knowledge.

Here we learn the precious lesson: *The whole aim of Christ's coming, the whole aim of redemption, the whole aim of Christ's work in our hearts is summed up in the one thought—"That God may be all in all."* We need to take this thought as our life motto. If we fail to see that this is Christ's object, we will never understand what He desires to work in us. But if we realize that everything must be subordinated to God the Father, then we have the same principle to rule our life that ruled the life of Christ. Let us meditate upon it with the earnest prayer: *Father, we hope to be present on that wondrous day when Christ shall give up the kingdom, and when you shall be all in all. We hope to be there to see it, to experience it, and to rejoice in it throughout eternity. Help us to know something of it now. Lord God, take your place and reveal your glory that our hearts may bow low, having but one song and one hope: that God may be all in all. Father, hear us, and may every heart be in submission to you. Amen.*

We have said this is why Jesus came into the world. This is the object of redemption. How does it relate to me? First, Christ, in His own life, realized that God the Father was all in all. He lived to please Him and to do His will. And so in our own lives, we can realize it too.

Christ realized and worked out our redemption. Looking at Christ, I see five steps to His life. (1) *His birth*; (2) *His life*; (3) *His death*; (4) *His resurrection*; and (5) *His ascension*.

1. *His birth.* He received His life from God. It was by an act of God's omnipotence that He was born of the Virgin Mary. It was from God that He had His mission, and He continually spoke of

being sent from God. Christ had His life from the Father and He always acknowledged it. This is the first thing a believer must learn from Christ. We should never view our conversion as something we have done, such as our repentance before God. Instead, we need to meditate in God's presence on the fact that just as it was the work of Almighty God to give His Son life here on earth, so God has given His life into our hearts. Our life is from God.

2. *His life.* The life Christ maintained on earth as a man was maintained in the power God gave Him. He said, "I can do nothing of myself." He always said that the words He spoke were the words the Father had given Him. He lived every moment of the day with the consciousness that God was absolutely all, and He was a vessel in which the Father could reveal His glory. That was the life of Christ—entire, unbroken, continuous dependence upon the Father; and His Father really was, in His life, every hour, *all in all.* That is what Christ came to show us.

Humankind was created to be a vessel into which God could pour His wisdom, goodness, beauty, and power. That is the heritage of the believer. It is God that makes the seraphim and cherubim flames of fire. The unrestricted glory of God passes through them. They are vessels prepared by God, come from God, that they might let God's glory shine through them.

And so it was with the Son. Sin entered—first, in the fallen angels, and then in man. The angels exalted themselves against God, would not receive the glory of God, and fell into "outer darkness." Eve listened to the serpent in the Garden, ate of the fruit, and gave some to Adam. Christ came to restore humankind. To do this He lived among us, day by day, depending upon His Father for everything. Even in His temptation in the wilderness, He would not touch a piece of bread until His Father gave it to

Him. Although He was hungry and had the power to turn a stone into bread, He would not eat until the Father sent the ministering angels. It is through this life of absolute dependence upon the Father that the glorified Christ will one day make sure that God is *all in all.*

3. *His death.* He not only received His life from God and lived it in dependence on God but He also yielded His life to God. He did it through complete obedience. Obedience is the surrendering of my will to the will of another. When a soldier bows to his general, or a scholar to his teacher, he is yielding his will—his life— he gives himself to the rule and mastery and the power of another. Christ did that. He said He came not to do His own will but to do His Father's will. In Gethsemane He said, "Take this cup from me. Yet not what I will, but what you will" (Mark 14:36). On the cross He suffered what had been settled in Gethsemane. He yielded His life to God and thereby taught us that the only thing worth living for is a life yielded to God, even unto death. If you are controlling your life and spending it on yourself, even partly, you are abusing it and taking it away from God's original purpose. Learn from Christ that the beauty and purpose of having life is so that you can surrender it to God and then allow Him to fill it with His glory.

Jesus surrendered His life through the Cross. But we must not look at crucifixion and death only from the side of sin. That is only half the truth. Why did Christ yield His life to death, and what did He gain by it? He gave up His earthly life, and God gave Him a heavenly life. He gave up the life of humiliation, and God gave Him a life of fellowship and glory. Do you desire the power and joy of a life that is in unbroken fellowship with God? There is only one way to have it. Surrender your life to God. That is what

Christ did. He yielded His life to death—into the hands of God. In the life of Christ, God the Father was everything. He was all in all.

4. *His resurrection.* Christ was raised from the dead. To understand the Resurrection, we must first ask what the Cross meant. What does giving up His life say to us? He yielded himself in utter helplessness to wait upon God. He always waited for His Father's instructions. The grave was His humiliation. There He waited until God the Father raised Him up to everlasting glory. Jesus' time in the grave was a very short time, yet it teaches us the lesson of fully surrendering our life into God's hands, to allow God to do all He wishes to do in us and through us. Surrender yourself in utter dependence upon God. Lose everything, and God will raise you up in glory. Christ could never have ascended to sit upon the throne, nor have accomplished His work of preparing the kingdom that He would give to the Father, if He had not begun by surrendering himself completely.

5. *His ascension.* The same principle holds true for Christ's ascension and entrance into glory.

Remember that the throne in heaven is not the throne of the Lamb of God alone; it is the throne of God the Father and the Lamb. Jesus went to share the throne with the Father; the Father was always first and Jesus second. Even on the throne of heaven, the glorified Lord Jesus honors the Father as Father. It is the deep mystery of the subordination of the Son to the Father. We must meditate upon it until we are full of this blessed truth: Even Jesus Christ lives in subordination to the Father, and because He sits in this spirit on the throne of glory, He will one day deliver the kingdom to the Father.

Consider this: The Lord Jesus came to remove the terrible

curse that sin had wrought, the awful ruin that had come through man's pride and self-exaltation; and He came to live out during thirty-three years on earth the fact that *God must be all in all.*

Did God disappoint Him? Not at all. God lifted Him to the throne of everlasting glory and to equality with himself, because He had humbled himself to honor God. Here we learn that the place of God's blessing is in humility and total dependence upon Him.

Are we called to live as Christ lived, that God may be all in all? Is Christ under any greater obligation to submit to God than we are? Many think so, but the Bible does not. The obligation, in fact, should be greater on us, for He is the Son of the Father and God with God; but we are created creatures. The sole purpose for our existence is that God might be "all in all," in us and to us. Have we understood it, expected it, sought for it? Have we ever learned to say with Christ: "It is worth yielding everything that God may have His rightful place"?

How can we attain to such a life? All our teaching about consecration is useless unless God becomes everything to us. What do we mean when we say, "Surrender yourselves as a living sacrifice"? First, this is not possible to do unless God is truly *all* in our life. Why is there so much complaining of weakness, failure, lost blessing, of walking in darkness? It can only be because God has not been given His rightful place in our lives. I ask you to pray with your whole heart that God would take first place in your life and that the inconceivable majesty of God may be so revealed that you will sink to your knees and say, "God, be all in my life, take all of my life, and use all that I am for your glory and praise." God help us to do this.

What are the steps to be taken by which we may be brought, in some measure, to live like Christ every day?

(1) *Take the time and effort to give God His place.* Study the Word; meditate upon God, the three persons of the Trinity; seek to discover the place that God desires to have in your life. Do not be content with the vague concept of a throne in the heavens where God sits and reigns. Remember, God is a Spirit. He not only sits on a throne, but He is present everywhere. He is revealed in nature, in the creation all around us, and how much more in the hearts of believers!

God is the fountain of all life. Every bit of life in the universe is the work of God. If you really give God His place, you will receive the humbling conviction that there is nothing but what has come from God; that God fills all things. The Bible says He works all in all, and so you will begin to say, "If God is everywhere and revealed in everything, I should see Him in nature, in providence, everywhere; I should always be seeing my God. When the believer sees God everywhere, he begins to give God His rightful place. He cannot rise in the morning without praising God and saying, "Lord God, you are glorious, you are everywhere, you are my life and the life of all living things." We pray because we believe in God and know something about God, but how little we comprehend who God is and how He is in control of all things!

Think of the place your pastor has in your church, your congregation. He guides and directs your meetings, he calls on his elders to pray or to speak; he may direct the singing and the Bible lessons; he may order the start of a building program or a missionary outreach. His is a small kingdom in his area of authority and ministry. He manages it, and you are grateful for it. But where is God in all of this? Yes, we thank God for our ministers, pastors, and leaders and for every earthly gift. But we must each learn to understand that in the church, in the prayer meeting, in our private devotions, we must allow God to take His place and bring glory to His name.

Will God do it? God is waiting to do it. *God longs to do it.* Just as one takes the place of the master or the mistress in your house and sits at the head of the table, supervises the children, and manages everything in an orderly, loving fashion, so God is willing to take the place of Master and loving God in our hearts and lives. Believers, have we given our glorious God the place He rightfully deserves? God forgive us if *we* have taken the place that Christ's redemption has given Him, and the place that Christ wants to have in us. Let us say in our deepest heart: "God shall have His place."

I might press still further in connection with the church. Does God have His full and rightful place there? Sadly, very seldom. May God help us to see this, and to motivate us to make the necessary changes.

So that is my first lesson: *Give God His place*; but know that it will take time and effort to do it. Listen and be quiet. The prophets said, "Let all flesh be silent before the Lord." And in 1 Corinthians 1:29: "That no flesh should glory in his presence" (KJV). We must give God time to reveal himself.

The second answer to the question, "How am I to attain this, that God may be all in all"? is: *Accept God's will in everything.*

Where do we find God's will? In His Word. I have often heard people say, Bible in hand, "I believe every word within these two covers has come from God"; and sometimes I have heard: "I want to believe every promise between these two covers"; but I have seldom heard it said, "I accept every commandment within these two covers." But we need to say it. Write in the front page of your

Bible: "Every promise of God in this book I intend to believe, every command of God in this book I purpose to obey." That is one step on the way to letting God be "all in all." Surrender your life to be the embodiment and expression of the will of God.

The second lesson is *Accept the will of God not only in the Bible but also in providence.* I find numbers of believers who have never learned that lesson. Do you know what it means? When Joseph's brothers sold him, he accepted God's hand in that, and despite the injustices that followed, we read, "God was with him." He was not separated from God when he was separated from his home and family. I read of David that when Shimei cursed him, he said, in effect, that he met God there in that cursing from Shimei, because God allowed it. When Judas came to kiss Christ and betray Him, when the soldiers bound Him, when Peter denied Him, when Caiaphas condemned Him, when Pilate gave Him over, Christ saw God His Father in everything. Therefore, Christ could drink the cup, for He saw the hand of His Father holding it.

Let us learn in every trial and trouble, great or small, to see God immediately. Meet your God there, and let God be who He is and allow Him to do what He does—all for your good and His glory. Not a hair of your head can fall without the will of your Father. Meet the will of your Father in every trial, in the deepest trial, the heaviest trial; the Son of God walks there. He is with you. And in the smallest trials—the person who irritates you, the child who hinders you, the friend who may have hurt you, the enemy who has reproached you, who has spoken evil of you and robbed you of your good name, the difficulty that worries you—why not say, *It is God who comes to me in every difficulty. I will meet Him, and honor Him, and give myself to Him. He will keep me!*

There are two great privileges in meeting God in a difficulty and knowing Him. The first is that even though the difficulty may have come through my own fault, if I confess it, then I can say, *God has allowed me to come into this situation, to come into this difficulty in order to teach me something. In this situation, God desires that I glorify Him.* And if God brings you into any difficulty by an act of someone else, you can count upon it that God will give you the grace to be humble and patient and to be perfected through the suffering or consequence, that in everything He may take His place. You will be able to look to Him with absolute confidence and say, *You have brought me here, and no one else, and you alone can take me out of it.* Nothing can separate you from the love of God in Christ Jesus. You have a wonderful place provided for you in His love. Learn to take this as the key out of every difficulty—*God is all in all.* And in prayer, day by day, make it your earnest supplication that God may be honored in every situation.

The third lesson is *Trust His almighty power.* Trust Him every day. If we could only begin to understand that our whole Christian life is to be the work of God himself. Paul speaks of it often: "For it is God who works in you to will and to act according to his good purpose" (Philippians 2:13). The will and the desire to obey—that is God's work in you, and that is only half of it. But He will work *to do,* as well as *to will,* if you will acknowledge Him in your life as *all.* In Hebrews we read: "May the God of peace . . . equip you with everything good for doing his will, and may he work in us what is pleasing to him" (13:20–21). Just as a watchmaker makes a watch—cuts it, cleans it, polishes it, and has put in every little wheel and spring—so the living God is actually and actively engaged in the work of perfecting your life every moment. You may ask, "If God is willing to work in my life every moment, why does He not work more powerfully?" The answer is simple: You do not yield to His power; you do not fully give Him His place; you do not wait upon Him to do it. Tell Him: "My God, here I am now. I give you your place in my life."

Suppose that when a painter came into his studio to paint an unfinished picture, the canvas had moved itself to some other part of the room. Until moved back to his easel, the painter could not paint. But suppose the canvas took on a voice and said: I will be still; come and do your work and paint your beautiful picture. Then the painter would come and do it. And if you say to God, "You are the mighty Workman, the wondrous Artist. I am still. Here I am. I trust your power and believe you." Then He will work wonders in you. God never works anything but wonders. That is His nature, even in what we call the laws of nature. Take the simplest thing—a blade of grass, or a little worm, or a flower; what wonders men of science tell us about them. And will not God work wonders in my heart and yours? He will. And why doesn't He do it more? Because we do not allow Him to. Learn to give Him His place, to accept His will, and then to trust His mighty work.

> In Thy strength I lay me down,
> Clay within the Potter's hands,
> Molded by Thy gentle will,
> Mightier than all commands:
> Moved and shaped by Thee alone,
> Now and evermore Thine own.

Is this little poem true of you? God is willing to mold you as really as the potter molds his clay. He will do it. Let us believe and trust His mighty power to do things above what we could ever ask or think. *God is waiting to do for you more than you can even conceive of.* Every yearning of your heart, every message that you have heard, of which you have said, "I wish I had that"; every prayer you have sent up—believe that God is willing to work it all in you and that He is waiting to do it. In every difficulty and every circumstance, God is there to work in you. Trust Him and honor Him and let Him be "all in all."

And then, once again, honor God, *sacrificing everything for His kingdom and glory.* If God is to be all in all, we must not come with the idea that I must be happy, and I must be holy, and I must have God's approval. The root principle of Christ's life was self-sacrifice to God for man. That is what He came for and it is a principle that every believer carries within him as unquenchable; but ... it can be smothered. Remember that your God longs to rule the world, and your Christ is upon the throne, desiring to lead you as His soldier and bless you with victory upon victory. Have you yielded yourself to God's glory? The soldier in an earthly army says, "Anything for my country, anything when my general leads me on to victory. I yield my home life and its comforts; I yield my life." Are earthly servants to have such devotion, and you and I merely *talk* about the glory of God and His being "all in all"? Can we afford to *talk* when we are called to help prepare the kingdom for Christ to give over to the Father, and when Christ tells us He is waiting for our help and depending upon it?

Instead, let us determine that God shall be "all in all"; I will sacrifice everything for Him. May God help us to make a fresh consecration of our whole being for the furtherance of Christ's kingdom. And whether it is in mission work in a foreign land or in Christian work close to home, whether we know how to work for Christ or not, let us yield ourselves as a willing sacrifice to be used for the glory of God.

Let this be your motto and watchword: *I will sacrifice everything and anything for the glory of my God.* And if you do not know what to sacrifice, ask Him. Be honest, be earnest, be simple, be childlike, and say, "Lord, every penny I have and every comfort I enjoy is yours. If you need it for your kingdom, I offer it to you." Let me ask you this: In eternity will anyone be sorry for having made himself poor in order to help bring about that majestic spectacle of the Son saying, "It is finished," and giving the kingdom to the Father, "that God may be all in all"? Do you hope to be there? Do you hope to have a share in the glory of that glorious scene? Are you willing to say, "Anything that I can do for your glory, Lord . . . here I am"? Surrender yourself to Him.

In conclusion, I want to leave one last thought: *Wait on God.*

It is one thing to speak and to think about God. But to know God in His glory within our souls, that is another thing. It is necessary to meditate and study, and try to form a right concept of the place God should occupy in your life. But that is not enough. You must do something else. I said, Yield yourselves to the will of God, prove the power of God, and seek the glory of God throughout the earth. But the most important step is to wait upon God.

This is because it is only God who can reveal himself. Remember that when God came to Adam, or Noah, or Abraham, or Moses, it was God who met them personally and showed himself in some form to them. That was under the old dispensation. And it still depends on the good pleasure of God to reveal himself. This is not an arbitrary good pleasure. It all depends upon whether He has found a heart hungering for Him. O that God would awaken that hunger and teach us to cry like David, "My soul thirsts for

God!" Wait upon God. Make that an increasing priority in your life. Perhaps we need to learn a lesson in quietness from the Quakers. In your private devotions, learn the secret of keeping silent before God with this one prayer, "Lord God, reveal yourself in the depths of my heart." And though you do not expect a vision, though you do not receive a manifestation—that is not what *should* be sought; it is that the soul should open itself to God and wait upon Him that He may come in. He is a God who sometimes withdraws himself. You cannot always see Him, but He will come in and take possession of you, revealing himself and working mightily in you, if you truly hunger for Him. *Wait upon God.* In your prayer meetings, let that be the first thing. It is to the detriment of both our private devotions and our prayer meetings that we begin to immediately pray as if all was right and in order. "Oh yes," we say, "God will do it"; and yet we fail to let our souls worship in holy awe and reverence and childlike trust. We do not take time to say, "Father, let it please you to come near and to meet with us."

The responsibility resting upon us is tremendous. Many of us sense we have received a secret for living the Christian life that other believers do not know about. We do not judge, but we confess that God has taught us something wonderful. Let us confess it boldly. But then, if that is true, we must come still nearer to God and have more of God in order to teach others how they can find God. You cannot find God without waiting upon Him. "Wait, I say, on the Lord."

If we take the steps given here, God will become our all in all. Then we will be prepared for taking our place in that glorious company who shall be present at that sublime, magnificent scene when Christ shall give up the kingdom to the Father—*that God may be all in all.*

Chapter 5

Set Apart for
the Holy Spirit

*In the church at Antioch there were prophets and teachers:
Barnabas, Simeon called Niger, Lucius of Cyrene, Manaen (who
had been brought up with Herod the tetrarch) and Saul. While
they were worshiping the Lord and fasting, the Holy Spirit said,
"Set apart for me Barnabas and Saul for the work to which I
have called them." So after they had fasted and prayed, they
placed their hands on them and sent them off. The two of them,
sent on their way by the Holy Spirit, went down
to Seleucia and sailed from there to Cyprus.*

Acts 13:1–4

Our purpose has been to discover the will of our God concerning
His work and to seek Him for the accompanying power. The story
of our text includes some precious thoughts to guide us concerning this. The great lesson of the verses is this: *The Holy Spirit is
the director of the work of God on earth.* If we are to work for God,
and if God is to bless our work, we must stand in a right relation
to the Holy Spirit. We must daily yield the place of honor that

belongs to Him, so that in all our work and in all our private inner life, the Holy Spirit shall always have the first place. Let me point out some of the particular thoughts our passage suggests.

First of all, we see that *God has His own plans regarding His kingdom.* His church at Antioch had been established. God had certain plans and intentions regarding Asia and Europe, and He made them known to His servants. Our great Commander organizes the campaign, but His generals and officers do not always know the great plans. They often receive sealed orders and have to wait on Him for what He gives them as orders. God in heaven has specific plans; we cannot doubt it. God has desires and a will with regard to the work that should be done and the way in which it is to be done. Blessed is the man who comes to know God's desires and works in harmony with God.

Some years ago at Wellington, we opened a missionary institute—housed in a fine large building. At our opening services the principal said something I have never forgotten. He remarked, "Last year we gathered here to lay the cornerstone, and what was here then? Nothing but rubbish, stones, bricks, and the ruins of an old building that had been torn down. There we laid the cornerstone, and very few knew what the building would be like when finished. In fact, no one knew it perfectly in every detail except one man, the architect. In his mind it was clear, and as the contractor, the mason, and the carpenter came to do their work, they simply took their orders from him. As the workers were obedient to instructions, the structure progressed as planned, and this beautiful building has been completed. Likewise," he added, "this building is but laying the foundation of a work of which only God knows the outcome." But God has His workers and His plans clearly mapped out; our position is to wait until God communicates to us as much of His will as is required for each moment.

We are simply to be faithful in obedience, carrying out His orders. God has a plan for His church on the earth. Unfortunately, we too often make our own plans and think that we know what should be done. We first ask God to bless our frail efforts instead of absolutely refusing to go ahead unless God goes before us. God has planned for the work and the extension of His kingdom. The Holy Spirit has this work as His responsibility. The work to be done by the church is Holy Spirit work. May God help us all to be afraid of touching "the ark of God" except as we are led by the Holy Spirit.

Then the _second_ thought is that _God is willing and able to reveal to His servants what His will is._ Yes, communications still come down from heaven. What the Holy Spirit said to the church in Antioch He will speak to His church and to His people today. He has often done it. He has come to individuals, and by His divine teaching has led them out into fields of labor that others could not at first understand or approve, into ways and methods that did not recommend themselves to the majority. But the Holy Spirit is still teaching His people. Thank God, in both our mission organizations and in our church work at home, in a thousand forms, the guiding of the Holy Spirit is known—but we are no doubt ready to confess: it is _too little_ known. We have not learned to wait upon Him enough to fully know His will.

Do not only ask God for power. Many believers have their own plan of serving, but God must send the power. They work in their own will and way and think that God must give the grace. This is why God so often gives so little grace and so little success. Let us take our place before God and say, "What is done in the will of God, will have the strength of God; what is done in the will of God must have God's blessing also." And so let our first desire be to have the will of God revealed.

If you ask whether it is easy to receive these communications from heaven, I can give you the answer. It is easy to those who are in right fellowship with God and who understand the art of waiting upon Him. How often have we asked how we can know the will of God? When people are perplexed, they pray earnestly that God would answer them at once. But God can reveal His will only to a heart that is humble and tender and quiet. God can reveal His will in perplexity and difficulty only to a heart that has learned to obey and honor Him in the small things of daily life.

This brings us to my *third* thought: What is the disposition to which the Spirit reveals God's will? What do we read in our text? There were a number of men ministering to the Lord and fasting when the Holy Spirit came and spoke to them. Some people understand this passage as compared to a missions committee meeting of our day. Our attention is brought to an open mission field, and we decide to begin a work there. We have virtually settled the fact, and then we pray about it. But our position is out of line. I doubt whether any of those in our text had considered Europe, for later on even Paul tried to go back into Asia until the night vision called him to the will of God. God had done wonders, extended the church to Antioch, and had given rich and large blessing. Here these men are ministering to the Lord, serving Him with prayer and fasting. They have a deep conviction: it must all come directly from heaven. We are in fellowship with the risen Lord; out of this close union with Him He will let us know what He wants. And there they were, quiet and waiting, glad and joyful, but deeply humbled. O Lord, they seem to say, we are your servants and in fasting and prayer we wait upon you. What is your will for us?

Was it not the same with Peter? He was on the housetop, fasting and praying, and not expecting the vision and command to go to Caesarea. He was ignorant of what his work might be. May God grant that this may become our position—our hearts entirely surrendered to the Lord Jesus, separated from the world and even from ordinary exercises of our Christian walk, and giving ourselves in intense prayer to look to our Lord. It is in such hearts that the will of God will be made known.

Notice that the word *fasting* occurs a second time (Acts 13:3): "They fasted and prayed." When you pray, you love to go into a private place, according to the command of Jesus, and shut the door. You shut out business, company, pleasure, anything that might distract your desire to be alone with God. Yet the material world follows you there. You must eat. These men desired to shut themselves out from the influences of the material and the visible, so they fasted. In the intensity of their souls, they gave expression to their letting go of everything on earth in their fasting before God. Oh, may God give us that intensity of desire, that separation from everything, because we desire to wait upon Him that the Holy Spirit may reveal to us His blessed will.

My *fourth* thought is this: *What has the Holy Spirit revealed concerning the will of God?* It is contained in our *being set apart to the Holy Spirit.* That is the keynote of the message from heaven. "Set apart for me Barnabas and Saul for the work to which I have called them." In effect, God said, This is mine and I care for it; I have chosen these men and called them, and I want you who represent the church of Christ on earth to set them apart unto me.

Look at this message in its twofold aspect. The men were to

be *set apart* to the Holy Spirit, and *the church was to do the separating work.* The Holy Spirit could trust these men to do it in a right spirit. They were abiding in fellowship with the Father and were under the leadership of the Holy Spirit. Because these were the men the Holy Spirit had prepared, He could say of them, "Set apart for me . . ."

This brings us to the very root of our need as servants of Christ. The question asked is "What is necessary for the power of God to rest upon us that the blessing of God should be poured out more abundantly among the lost among whom we labor?" The answer is "I want men separated to the Holy Spirit." What does this imply? Christ said, when He spoke about the Holy Spirit, "The world cannot receive Him." Paul said, "We have received not the spirit of the world, but the Spirit that is of God." That is the great need in every servant—the spirit of the world being displaced by the incoming Spirit of God, who takes possession of the inner life and of the whole being.

No doubt many of us often cry to God for the Holy Spirit to come upon us as a Spirit of power for our work, and when we feel that measure of power, we thank God for it. But God desires something more, something higher. God desires that we seek for the Holy Spirit as a Spirit of power in our own heart and life to conquer self and cast out sin and to work the blessed and beautiful image of Jesus into us.

There is a difference between the power of the Spirit as a gift and the power of the Spirit for the grace of a holy life. A man may often have a measure of the power of the Spirit, but if He does not rule the heart as the Spirit of grace and of holiness, the lack will be seen in his work. The man may have been effective in evangelism, but he will never help people onto a higher standard of spiritual life. And when he dies, a great deal of his work may pass away too. But a man who is separated to the Holy Spirit is a man who says, "Father, let the Holy Spirit have full dominion over me—in my home, in my disposition, and in every word of my tongue, in every thought of my heart, in every attitude toward others; let the Holy Spirit have entire possession of me." Has that been the desire and the covenant of your heart with your God— to be a man or a woman separated and yielded to the Holy Spirit? Look at the text again. The Holy Spirit said, "Set apart for me . . ." May God grant that the Word may enter into the very depths of our being to search us, and if God reveals to us that the self-life, self-will, and self-exaltation are there, may we humble ourselves before Him. Let us fully separate ourselves from the world.

It is necessary that we take time to kneel before God and to ask Him to humble us under His mighty hand. Whoever you are in the body of Christ, you are a servant set apart to the Holy Spirit. Have you acknowledged this by faith? Are you living with this reality? Has that been your expectation from our risen and almighty Lord Jesus? If not, may God write the word in our hearts!

I said the Holy Spirit spoke to the church at Antioch as a church capable of doing His work. The Holy Spirit trusted them. May God grant that our churches, our mission organizations, our Sunday schools, our Bible colleges may be equipped with pastors, directors, teachers, councils, committees, and layworkers who believe in the power and enabling of the Holy Spirit to do their work.

My *fifth* thought is that *this partnership with the Holy Spirit in His work becomes a matter of conscious action.* The men in the church at Antioch set apart Paul and Barnabas, and then it is written of the two that they, being sent forth by the Holy Spirit, went down to Seleucia and sailed from there to Cyprus. The Holy Spirit does His part of the work, and we are commissioned to do our part. After the ordination of the men on earth, it is written in God's inspired Word that they were sent forth by the Holy Spirit.

We see how this partnership calls us to fresh prayer and fasting. They had been fasting and ministering to the Lord for a certain time, perhaps days; the Holy Spirit gave the directions for the work and immediately they came together for more prayer and fasting. That is the spirit in which they obeyed the command of their Lord. It teaches us that it is not only in the beginning of our Christian work, but all along the way that we need to receive our strength through prayer. If there is one thought with regard to the church that comes to me with overwhelming sorrow, one thought in regard to my own life of which I am ashamed, and one thought that I feel the church has not accepted or grasped fully: *it is the wonderful power that prayer is meant to have in the kingdom*—and we have so little availed ourselves of it!

You may have read the expression of Christian in John Bunyan's great work *Pilgrim's Progress,* when he found he had the key in his breast that would unlock the dungeon. We have this key that can unlock the world of heathendom around us. But *we are far more occupied with our work than we are with prayer.* We believe more in speaking to strangers than we believe in speaking to God. Learn from these early Christians that the work that the Holy Spirit commands must call us to fresh fasting and prayer, to new separation from the spirit and the pleasures of the world to new consecration to God and to His fellowship. Those men yielded themselves to fasting and prayer, and if in our everyday Christian work there were more prayer, there would be more blessing in our inner life. If we were convinced that our only strength is to be found in abiding every moment with Christ, every moment allowing God to work in us—if that were our spirit, wouldn't our lives be holier? Wouldn't they be more fruitful?

There are few warnings in God's Word more solemn than what we find in Galatians 3, where Paul asked, "After beginning with the Spirit, are you now trying to attain your goal by human effort?" Do you understand what that means? There is the danger in Christian work, just as in our Christian life, that is begun with much prayer and in the Holy Spirit, of a gradual straying off to the ways of the flesh and dependence upon our own strength. In our beginning perplexity and helplessness we prayed often to God; God answered and blessed; our walk and our work was perfected and our faith enlarged; but gradually daily life and daily work so took possession of us that the power of the Spirit was nearly lost completely. So let us take note and remember, the early church was launched in service with fresh prayer and fasting, and with more prayer and fasting, so that this company of disciples carried out the command of the Holy Spirit. To wait on God is our highest and most important work. The Holy Spirit comes in answer to believing prayer.

You will remember that when the exalted Jesus ascended to the throne, the footstool of the throne was for ten days the place where His waiting disciples cried to Him. And that is the law of the kingdom: the King upon the throne, the servants upon His footstool, calling upon Him. May God find us there unceasingly.

My *final* thought is of *the wonderful blessing that comes when the Holy Spirit is allowed to direct Christian work and when it is carried on in obedience to Him.* You know the story of the mission on which Barnabas and Saul were sent. You know what power there was with them. The Holy Spirit sent them, and they went on from place to place with great blessing. The Holy Spirit was their leader from then on. You remember that the Spirit hindered Paul from going again into Asia and instead led him into Europe. Oh, the blessing that rested on that small company of men and upon their ministry!

The secret is to truly believe that God has so much blessing for us. The Holy Spirit, into whose hands God has put the work, has been called "the executive of the Holy Trinity." The Holy Spirit has not only the power but is the Spirit of love. He is brooding over this dark world and every sphere of work within it. He is willing to bless. Why is there not more blessing? There can only be one answer. We have not honored the Holy Spirit as we should. Can anyone say it is not true? Is not every thoughtful heart honest in saying, "God, forgive me that I have not honored the Holy Spirit, that I have grieved Him, that I have allowed my flesh and my own will to work where the Holy Spirit should have been allowed to work." Our sin is greater than we know! It is no wonder there is so much weakness and failure in the church.

Chapter 6

Peter's Repentance

The Lord turned and looked straight at Peter. Then Peter
remembered the word the Lord had spoken to him: "Before the
rooster crows today, you will disown me three times."
And he went outside and wept bitterly.

Luke 22:61–62

This was the turning point in Peter's life. Christ had said to him, "You cannot follow me now." Peter was not able to follow Christ, because he had not come to the end of himself. But when he realized what he had done and how Christ's prophecy of his actions had come true, he went out and wept bitterly. At this point, the great change came about. Jesus had previously said to him, "When you are converted, strengthen your brethren." At the place of this new revelation of himself, Peter was converted from self to Christ.

I thank God for the story of Peter. I know no other man in the Bible who gives greater comfort to the human frame. When we look at his character, so full of failures, and at what Christ made him by the power of the Holy Spirit, there is hope for every one of us. But remember, before Christ could fill Peter with the Holy Spirit and make a new creation of him, Peter had to acknowledge his frailty and his wrongdoing; he had to be humbled. To understand this, there are four points to consider: (1) *Peter the devoted disciple of Jesus*; (2) *Peter as he lived the life of self*; (3) *Peter in his repentance*; and (4) *Peter's deliverance from self*.

(1) *Peter the devoted disciple of Jesus.* Christ called Peter to leave his fishing nets and follow Him. Peter did so at once and afterward could truthfully say, "We have forsaken all, and followed you." Peter was a man of *entire surrender*; he surrendered all to follow Jesus. Peter was also a man of *true obedience.* You remember that Christ said to him, "Launch out into the deep, and let down the net." Peter, an experienced fisherman, knew there were no fish there; they had been struggling all night and had caught nothing. But he said, "At your word I will let down the net." He submitted to the word of Jesus. Further, he was a man of *great faith.* When he saw Christ walking on the water, he said, "Lord, if it is you, bid me come to you"; and at the voice of Christ he stepped out of the boat and walked on the water. Peter was also a man of *spiritual insight.* When Christ asked the disciples, "Who do you say I am?" Peter answered, "You are the Christ, the Son of the living God." And Christ said, "Blessed are you, Simon son of Jonah, for this was not revealed to you by man, but my Father in heaven." (See Matthew 16:15–19.) Christ spoke of him as the "rock" and of his having the keys to the kingdom. Peter was a splendid friend and a devoted disciple of Jesus. And yet how much was still lacking in Peter!

(2) *Peter as he lived the life of self.* He pleased himself, trusted himself, and sought honor for himself. Not unlike us before death to self. Just after Christ had said to Peter, "This was not revealed to you by man, but my Father in heaven," Christ began to speak about His sufferings. Peter dared to say, "Never, Lord! This shall

never happen to you!" Then Christ had to say, "Get behind me, Satan! You are a stumbling block to me; you do not have in mind the things of God, but the things of men." There was Peter in his self-will, trusting his own wisdom, and actually forbidding Christ to die. What prompted this? Peter trusted himself and his own thoughts about divine things. We see later on, more than once, that when the disciples were questioning among themselves who should be the greatest, Peter was one of them. He thought he had a right to the very first place. He sought his own honor even above the others. The life of self was strong in Peter.

When Christ had spoken to him about His sufferings and said, "Get behind me, Satan," He followed it up by saying, "If anyone would come after me, he must deny himself and take up his cross and follow me." No man can follow Him unless he does that. Self must be utterly denied. What does this mean? When Peter denied Christ, three times he said he didn't know the man. In other words, "I have nothing to do with Him; He and I are not friends; I deny having any connection with Him." Christ told Peter that he must deny himself. Self must be ignored and its every claim rejected. That is the root of true discipleship; but Peter did not understand it and could not obey it. Consequently, when the last night came, Christ said to him, "Before the rooster crows today, you will disown me three times." But with what self-confidence Peter said, "Lord, I am ready to go with you to prison and to death." Peter truly meant it and really intended to do it; but Peter didn't know himself.

Perhaps we do not know ourselves so well either. Do we give place to our self-life? What have we done with our flesh, entirely under the power of sin? Deliverance from that is what we need.

Peter did not understand this, and therefore in self-confidence he even denied his Lord.

Notice how Christ used that word *deny* twice. He said to Peter the first time, *Deny yourself;* and the second time, *You will deny me* (*disown,* as some translations have it). It is either one or the other. There is no alternative; we must either deny self or deny Christ. There are two great powers fighting each other—the self-life in the power of sin, and Christ in the power of God. One of these must rule within us.

(3) *Peter in his repentance.* Peter had denied the Lord three times before the Lord looked at him; that look of Jesus must have broken Peter's heart. His look exposed the terrible sin that Peter had committed—the terrible failure that had come, the depth into which he had fallen, and "Peter went outside and wept bitterly."

Who can tell what that repentance must have been? During the following hours of that night and the next day, when he saw Christ crucified and buried, and the next day, the Sabbath—what hopeless despair and shame he must have experienced that day! "My Lord is gone, my hope is gone, and I denied Him! After that life of love, after the blessed fellowship we had for three years, I denied my Lord. God, have mercy upon me!" I don't think it is possible to imagine into what depths of humiliation Peter sank. But that was the turning point and the change; on the first day of the week Christ was seen by Peter, and in the evening He met him with the others. Later on at the Lake of Galilee He asked him, "Do you love me?" until Peter was saddened again by the thought that he had denied Him. He said in sorrow, but in honesty, "Lord, you know all things; you know that I love you."

(4) *Peter's deliverance from self.* As we know, Christ took Peter with the others to the footstool of the throne and told him to wait

there; on the Day of Pentecost the Holy Spirit came, and Peter was a changed man. We usually only detect the change in Peter in the boldness and power, the insight into the Scriptures, and the blessing with which he preached on that day. But there was something deeper and better for Peter. Peter's whole nature was changed.

If you want to see it, read the first epistle of Peter. You know Peter's former tendencies to fail. When he said to Christ, in effect, "You must never suffer; it cannot be"—it showed he had not understood what it was to pass through death into life. Christ said, "Deny yourself," and in spite of that Peter denied his Lord. When Christ warned him, "You will deny me," and he insisted that he never would, Peter showed how little he understood himself. But when I read his epistle and hear him say, "If you suffer as a Christian, do not be ashamed, but praise God that you bear that name" (4:16) then I know it is not the old Peter but the very Spirit of Christ breathing and speaking through him. When I read how he says, "Do not be surprised at the painful trial you are suffering, as though something strange were happening to you. But rejoice that you participate in the sufferings of Christ, so that you may be overjoyed when his glory is revealed," I understand what a change has come over Peter. Instead of denying Christ, he found joy and pleasure in denying self, even giving it over to death. Therefore, in Acts we read that when he was called before the council, he could boldly say, "We must obey God rather than men"; he could return with the other disciples and rejoice that they were counted worthy to suffer for Christ's name. And so dear readers, I ask you, look at Peter utterly changed—the self-pleasing, self-trusting, self-seeking Peter filled with the Spirit and the life of Jesus. Christ changed him by the Holy Spirit.

So what is my object in having briefly pointed to the story of Peter? It is the story of every servant who will be truly used by God. Peter's story is a prophecy of what each of us can receive from God. We must not only pray for God's work and talk about it; not only pray for an outpouring of the Spirit of love and that God would bind us together in the power of love; but we must come to God as individuals. For it is when individual servants are blessed that the work will prosper and the body will be strong and healthy.

Let us briefly summarize the lessons in Peter's life:

(1) *It is possible to be a very earnest, godly, devoted, and to some extent, successful worker in whom the power of the flesh is still very strong.*

This is a certain fact, and only God knows the depth of it in our service. Peter, before he denied Christ, had cast out demons and healed the sick. There are many who have been serving God with success and praise Him for the blessing; and yet, like in Peter, the flesh has significant freedom and power. What we must realize is that because there is so much self-life in us, the power of God cannot work in us as mightily as He desires to. Do you realize that God is longing to multiply His blessings through us? But there is something hindering Him, and it is nothing less than the self-life. We talk about the pride of Peter, the impulsiveness of Peter, the self-confidence of Peter. But we are all guilty of the same behavior. It is all rooted in that one word *self*. When Christ said, "Deny yourself," Peter did not understand or obey the command—every failure came out of that.

And so there may be servants of God—pastors, leaders of large ministries, people of power and position and talent, or ordinary layworkers—working earnestly for God, in whom the self-life prevails. It is something to think about. It has happened to many a Christian who has worked for many years in the church, perhaps occupying a prominent position, to whom God has revealed the inner life, and he has become utterly ashamed and broken before God. Peter went out and wept bitterly, and there may be the same reaction in those who find that they have failed to honor God in the presence of others.

(2) *It is the work of our blessed Lord Jesus to reveal to us the power of self.*

How was it that Peter, strong-willed and full of himself, ever became a man of Pentecost and the writer of his epistle? It was because he was a disciple of Christ; Christ had cared for him, taught him many wonderful things, and blessed him. The admonitions Christ gave him were part of the training; even that last look of love, when Peter had betrayed Him. Even in His suffering, Christ did not forget Peter. The same Christ who led Peter to Pentecost is among us today and is waiting to take charge of every heart that is willing to surrender to Him.

Are you at that place today? Are you saying, "This is my problem; it is always the self-life, the self-comfort, the self-consciousness, the self-pleasing, and the self-will; how can I free myself from it?" The only answer is: Christ Jesus can free you; Christ Jesus can deliver you from the power of self. He only asks that you humble yourself before Him.

Chapter 7

Absolute Surrender

Now Ben-Hadad king of Aram mustered his entire army.
Accompanied by thirty-two kings with their horses and chariots,
he went up and besieged Samaria and attacked it. He sent
messengers into the city to Ahab king of Israel, saying,
"This is what Ben-Hadad says: 'Your silver and gold are mine,
and the best of your wives and children are mine.'"
The king of Israel answered, "Just as you say,
my lord the king. I and all I have are yours."

1 Kings 20:1–4

What Ben-Hadad asked for was *absolute surrender*; what Ahab gave what was asked of him—*absolute surrender*. I want to use these words—"Just as you say, my lord the king. I and all I have are yours"—as the words of absolute surrender every believer should render to God. We have stated it before, but it bears repeating: The absolute surrender of everything into His hands is necessary. If our hearts are willing for that, there is no limit to what God will do for us or to the blessing He will bestow.

"Absolute surrender"—let me tell you where I discovered this term. I have used it often, and you may be familiar with it. Some time ago, in Scotland, I was discussing the condition of the church with a group of Christian workers. In our group there was a godly man whose main ministry was that of training others in Christian service. I asked him what he thought was the greatest need of the church and the message that should be preached. He answered very quietly and simply, but determinedly: "Absolute surrender to God is the main thing." The words struck me as never before. He went on to tell me that if the workers he trains are sound on that one point, even though they may be lacking in some areas, they are teachable and always improve; whereas those who are not totally surrendered, very often go back on their commitment and leave the work. The condition for obtaining God's full blessing is *absolute surrender* to Him.

I desire by God's grace to make this point unquestionably clear: God answers your prayers for spiritual blessing with this one requirement: the willingness to surrender yourself absolutely into His hands. God knows the hearts of those who have done it and of those who long to do it but still have doubts or fears. Then there are those who have said they surrendered, but have miserably failed, and who feel condemned because they have not found the secret of the power to live a consecrated life.

Let me say, first of all, *God requires it of us.* It has its foundation in the very nature of God. God cannot do otherwise. God is the Fountain of Life, the only Source of existence, power, and goodness. Throughout the universe there is nothing good unless God is in it. God has created all that we see around us of nature. It is all absolutely surrendered to Him in the sense that God works in creation just as He pleases. When God clothes the lily with its beauty, is it not yielded, surrendered, to God? It has no power in itself to control its beauty, its life, or its death. As God's redeemed children, do you imagine that God can accomplish His work in you if there is only half or a part of your life surrendered to Him? *He cannot.* God is life, love, blessing, power, and infinite beauty, and He delights to communicate himself to every believer who is prepared to receive Him; but any lack of absolute surrender will hinder God. Still He comes to you and claims what is due Him.

You know in daily life what absolute surrender is. You know that everything has to be committed to its particular purpose and service. I have a pen in my pocket that is surrendered to its purpose of writing and must be surrendered to my hand if I am to write with it properly. If someone else has a partial hold on it, I cannot write with it. My coat is absolutely yielded to me to cover my body. It is its purpose. A building may be entirely yielded to church services. And do you expect that in your immortal being, in the divine nature that you have received by regeneration, God can accomplish His work without your having entirely surrendered to Him? *It is not possible.* The temple of Solomon was absolutely surrendered to God when it was dedicated to Him. And each of us is a temple of God in which God will dwell and work mightily on one condition: absolute surrender to Him. God claims it, God is worthy of it, and without it God cannot accomplish His blessed work in us.

Second, *God not only claims it, He will work it out.* I am sure many believers say, "Absolute surrender implies so much!" Recently I received a note from someone that read, "I have experienced so much trial and suffering, and there is so much of the self-life still remaining; I dare not face entire surrender, because I know it will cause even more trouble and agony." Can it be that believers have such thoughts of Him? I come to you with this message: God does not ask you to make a full surrender in your own strength or by the power of your will; God wants to help you. "It is God that works in us, both to will and to do of His good pleasure." And that is our great need—to go to our knees before God until our hearts learn to believe that the everlasting God himself will come into our lives to change what is wrong, to conquer what is evil, and to work what is well-pleasing in His sight. God himself will work it in you.

Look at the men in the Old Testament. Do you think it was by accident that God found a man like Abraham, the father of the faithful and the friend of God? Do you think it was Abraham himself, apart from God, who had such faith and obedience and devotion? You know that is not so. God raised him up and prepared him as an instrument for His glory. God said to Pharaoh, "For this cause have I raised you up, to show my power in you." And if God said that of him, will He not say it of every child of His? I want to encourage you to cast out every fear. Come with your meager desire, and if there is fear that it is not strong enough to make your surrender, realize that God can make you willing, if you ask Him. If there is anything holding you back, or any sacrifice you are afraid to make, come to God and prove how gracious He is. He will never command of you what He will not enable you to do! God offers to work this absolute surrender in you. All the searching, hungering, and longing in your heart is a result of His work. He who lived a life of absolute surrender is living in your heart by His Holy Spirit. You may have hindered Him in the past, but He purposes through your humiliation and waiting upon Him to help you find the place of full surrender.

Third, *God not only requires our surrender and works it in us, but God accepts it when we bring it to Him.* Remember, when you do come with what you think is your absolute surrender, it may, as far as your feelings go, be imperfect. You may doubt and hesitantly say, "Is it absolute?" But remember the man to whom Christ said, "If you can believe, all things are possible to him that believes"; his heart was afraid and he cried out, "Lord, I believe, help my unbelief." That was a faith that triumphed over the Evil One. If you come and say, "Lord, I yield myself in absolute surrender to you," even though it may be with a trembling heart and without feeling—"I do not feel the power; I do not feel the determination; I do not feel the assurance"—your surrender will be received. Do not be afraid to come just as you are, and even in the midst of your trembling, the power of the Holy Spirit will work.

The Holy Spirit works with mighty power even when on the human side everything appears weak. Look at the Lord Jesus Christ in Gethsemane. We read that He, "through the Eternal Spirit," offered himself as a sacrifice to God. The Almighty Spirit of God was enabling Him to do it. And yet what agony and fear and exceeding sorrow came over Him as He prayed! Externally you can see no sign of the mighty power of the Spirit, but the Spirit of God was there. Even so, while you are weak and struggling and fearful, through faith in the hidden work of God's Spirit, yield yourself. The first step in absolute surrender is to believe that God accepts your surrender. That is a point we often miss. Be occupied with God, not yourself, in your commitment to Him. We want God to be present with us in our daily life, to have the right place, to be all in all. To experience this, we must look away from ourselves and to God. Though you may feel inadequate and unworthy, full of failure and sin and fear, bow before Him in simplicity and say, "O God, I accept your terms; I have pleaded for blessing on myself and others. I have accepted your terms of absolute surrender." While your heart speaks this deep within, God takes note of it and writes it down in His book; God is present at that very moment and takes complete possession of you. You may not feel it, you may not realize it, but trust Him. Who can estimate the work that can be done in and through the church if we would individually and collectively say, "I make an absolute surrender to God."

Fourth, *God not only claims my surrender, accepts it when I offer it, but He maintains it as well.* This is a great difficulty with many. People say, "I have often been moved at a meeting and have consecrated myself to God, but it has always dissipated. It may last for a week or a month, but it fades away and after a time is completely gone."

It does not have to be this way. When God has begun the work of absolute surrender in you by accepting your offer of surrender, He promises to care for it and to keep it. Do you believe this?

In this matter of surrender, both *God and I* are involved—I am unworthy and inadequate; God is the everlasting and omnipotent Jehovah. Unworthy one, are you afraid to trust yourself to this mighty God? God is willing. One of God's servants recently pleaded in prayer that each of us might hear His voice asking us, *"Do you believe that I can do this, that I can keep you continually, day by day, and moment by moment?"* Remember the beautiful chorus:

Moment by moment I'm *kept* in His love;
Moment by moment I've life from above.

If God allows the sun to shine upon you moment by moment, without intermission, will not God let His life shine upon you every moment? And why have you not experienced it? Because you have not trusted God for it or you do not surrender yourself absolutely to God in that trust.

A life of absolute surrender has its difficulties. I do not deny that. Yes, it has something far more than difficulties; it is a life that with humankind is absolutely impossible. But by the grace of God, by the power of the Holy Spirit dwelling in us, it is a life to which we are destined and that is possible for us, praise God! Let us believe that God will maintain it. Perhaps you have read the words of George Müller who, on his ninetieth birthday, told of all God's goodness to him. What did he say was the secret of his happiness and of all the blessings that God had given him? He said he believed there were two reasons. The one was that he had been enabled by grace to maintain a clear conscience before God day by day; the other was that he was a lover of God's Word. Yes, a clear conscience in sincere obedience to God day by day, and fellowship with God every day in His Word and prayer—that is a life of absolute surrender.

Such a life has two sides—on the one side, *absolute surrender to do what God wants me to do*; on the other side, *to allow God to work in me what He wants to do.*

On the one side, *to do what God wants me to do.* Surrender yourselves absolutely to the will of God. You may not know everything about God's will, but with what you do know, say to the Lord, "By your grace I desire to do your will in everything, every moment of every day." Say, "Lord God, I desire not a word upon my tongue but for your glory, not a movement of my temper but for your glory, not an emotion of love or hate in my heart but for your glory and according to your blessed will." Someone says, "Do you think that is possible?" I ask, "What has God promised? What can God do with a vessel absolutely surrendered to Him?" God waits to bless us in a way beyond what we expect. "It is written, eye has not seen, nor ear heard, neither have entered into the heart of man, the things which God has prepared for them that love Him." God has prepared unheard-of things, things you could never think of; blessings much more wonderful than you could imagine, more mighty than you could conceive. They are divine blessings. Come and say, "I give myself absolutely to God, to His will, to do only what God wants." It is God who will enable you to carry out your surrender.

On the other side, say, "I give myself absolutely to God, *to allow Him to work in me to will and to do of His good pleasure,* as He has promised to do." Yes, the living God wants to work in believers in a way that we cannot understand, but that is what God's Word has revealed, and He wants to work in us every moment of the day. God is willing to maintain our life; only let our absolute surrender be one of simple, childlike, and unbounded trust.

Fifth, *Our absolute surrender to God will result in wonderful blessing.* Remember what Ahab said in our opening text to his enemy King Ben-Hadad: "Just as you say, my lord the king. I and all I have are yours." Shall we not say this to our God and loving Father? If we do say it, God's blessing will come upon us. God calls you to be separate from the world and sin. If we say in all sincerity that all we have and are belong to Him, He will accept it and teach us what it means.

I say again, God will bless you. Have you been praying for blessing? Remember, there must be absolute surrender. God cannot fill you and bless you without it. Absolute surrender is what our souls must yield by divine grace.

Humble yourselves in God's sight and acknowledge that you

have grieved the Holy Spirit by your self-will, self-confidence, and self-effort. Bow humbly before Him in that confession and ask Him to break your heart and to bring you to your knees before Him. Then as you bow before Him, receive God's Word that says in your flesh "there dwells no good thing" and that nothing will help you except another life, which must enter yours. You must deny self once and for all. Denying self must every moment be the power of your life, and then Christ will come in and take possession of you.

When was Peter delivered? When was the change accomplished? It began when Peter wept over his sin; then the Holy Spirit came and filled his heart. God the Father loves to give us the power of the Spirit. We have the Spirit of God dwelling within us. We come to God confessing that and praising God for it; and yet confessing how we have grieved the Spirit. And then we bow our knees to the Father to ask that He would strengthen us with all might by the Spirit in the inner man, and that He would fill us with His mighty power. As the Spirit reveals Christ to us, Christ comes to live in our hearts forever, and the self-life is cast out.

As we bow before God in our own humiliation, we will want to also confess before Him the condition of the whole church. No words can fully express our sadness. I wish I had words to speak what I sometimes feel about it. Just think of the believers around you. I am not speaking of nominal Christians or of those professing faith, but I speak of those honest, sincere believers who are not living a life in the full power of God or to His glory. So little power, so little devotion or consecration to God, so little concept of the truth that a believer is one utterly surrendered to God's will! We will want to confess the sins of God's people around us and to humble ourselves. We are members of a sick body, and the sickliness of the body will hinder and break us down, unless we come to God and in confession separate ourselves from partnership with worldliness, with coldness toward each other, unless we surrender ourselves wholly to God.

How much is being done in the spirit of the flesh and in the power of self! How much work, day by day, in which human energy—our will and our thoughts about the work—is continually manifested and in which there is very little waiting upon God for the power of the Holy Spirit! Let us make confession. But as we confess the weakness and sinfulness of work for God among us, let us come back to ourselves. Do you truly desire to be delivered from the power of the self-life? Have you acknowledged the power of self and the flesh and been willing to cast it all at the feet of Christ? *There is deliverance.*

Remember: Death was the path to glory for Christ. For the joy set before Him He endured the cross. The cross was the birthplace of His everlasting glory. Do you love Christ? Do you long to be *in* Christ and not merely *like* Him? Let death be to you the most desirable thing on earth—death to self and fellowship with Christ. Separation—do you think it a hard thing to be entirely free from the world and by that separation be united to God and His love, by separation to become prepared for living and walking with God every day? Surely we should say, "Anything to bring me to separation, to death, for a life of full fellowship with God and Christ." Come and cast this self-life and flesh-life at the feet of Jesus. Then trust Him. Do not try to understand it all, but come in the living faith that Christ will come into you with the power of His death and the power of His life; then the Holy Spirit will bring the whole Christ—Christ crucified and Christ risen and living in glory—into your heart.

Chapter 8

Christ Our Life

When Christ, who is your life, appears, then you also
will appear with him in glory.

Colossians 3:4

I know that many who have made an absolute surrender have felt as I have felt: O God, how little we understand it! And they have prayed, "Lord God, you must truly take possession if we are to know what it really means." It has been stated that we believe that through our faith God does accept our surrender, although the experience and the power of that absolute surrender may not come at once, and that we are to hold fast our faith in God until the experience and power do come.

But let me now add what has only been mentioned before: *If this absolute surrender is to be maintained and lived out, it must be by having Christ come into our life in new power.* That is the thought I wish to address now. It is only in Christ that we can draw near to God, and it is only in Christ that God can draw near to us. Christ is our life. We often plead with God to work mightily in the church and in the world, in the power of the Holy Spirit for the sanctification of His people and for the conversion of sinners. What we need is that *what we ask God to do in others would be done also in ourselves.* We need to allow Christ to take entire possession of us, and then Christ will be able to work through us above what we ask or think.

To illustrate this great truth of "Christ our life," I want to use four very simple thoughts. If we want to understand those words, let us consider, first, *Christ our example*; second, *Christ our propitiation*; third, *Christ our Savior from sin*; and finally, *Christ our strength and our life.*

O Lord, give your grace that these human words may not cover us with any covering but the covering of your Spirit. Lord God, awaken in our hearts the realization that we are all children of your family, bowing before your feet. Awaken in every heart a deep faith that our God, by the Holy Spirit, is going to reveal Christ to us even now. Our Father, we wait on you. Our soul waits and our hope is in your Word.

If Christ is to be our life, we must first look at *Christ as our example.* When I speak of Christ as my life, it must not be a vague generalization. Life always works itself out in conduct and action; if Christ comes into me as my life, He must not be hidden in my heart, but a presence that proves himself in every action and in every moment of my existence. If I want to know how it will be, what my attitudes and words and actions and habits will be if I have Christ's life, I must study the life of the Lord Jesus on earth. As I study the life and walk of God's beloved Son, I must remember that one of the reasons God sent Jesus to live on the earth was so that I might have a picture, a revelation, a representation of what God wanted me to be and was willing to make me. That is the light in which we should study the life of Christ in the Gospels—not the only light, but perhaps the most important light.

What do I find as I look at Christ? I find absolute surrender to God. That was the very root of His life. He came as a man whom God had sent into the world, and as a man whose only purpose was to fulfill the will of God. He came as a man who had nothing in himself, but who every day depended upon God and waited for God to teach Him, to speak words through Him, and to show Him the works He had to do. "The Son can do nothing of himself." He lived a life of absolute surrender to God. God's will, God's honor, and God's kingdom—He lived and He died for them. He did not do it only at certain times, casting off responsibility at other times to seek relaxation in something of the world and forgetting to hold communion with God, as many believers today do. The Christian walk is often seen as a burden or a duty, and it is a relief just to relax a little and throw off the strain. But God the Father was Christ's joy and the fountain of living waters to Him; it was His delight and His strength to live in God and for God. The will of God was His meat and refreshment and strength.

And God comes to all of us who are asking, "My God, I have made an absolute surrender to you, and you know that although it was done in weakness and trembling, it was done in honesty and uprightness; but, my God, what does it mean? How am I to live that life?" The Father points to the beloved Son and says, "This is my beloved Son, in whom I am well pleased. Hear Him, follow Him, live like Him, let Christ be the law of your life."

Let us yield our hearts to God in prayer that He might search and reveal to us whether the life of Christ has actually been the law of our life. I am not speaking about attainment, but whether we have actually said, "How blessed it would be! This is what I desire and wait upon God for! It almost sounds too high or too presumptuous." But what did Christ mean when He said, "As I have loved you, even so love one another; as I kept the commandments of my Father, so, if you keep His commandments, you will abide in my love"? What does the Holy Spirit mean when He says, "Let this mind be in you, which was also in Christ Jesus . . . who made himself of no reputation . . . but humbled himself, and became obedient unto death"? The mind of Christ must be my mind, my disposition, and my life.

Many people want eternal life but do not want to live the life here on earth that Christ lived. There are many believers who have said, "There is no possibility of imitating or following Christ with any degree of perfection." Their goal is not to come near to Christ. But if you have honestly given your heart in surrender to God, you must admit, the life of Christ must become yours.

Second, if we want to know what "Christ our life" means, we must not only look at Christ and His work as our example, but *Christ for us as our propitiation.* During His life on earth, Christ prepared the path in which we are to walk. He left us an example that we should follow in His footsteps; He marked out the road we were to travel on the way to eternal life. But that was not enough, for we were shut out from the path and that life by sin and death. And so Christ, after having prepared and marked out the blessed path, suffered the agony and death of Calvary, yielding His will to God unto the end. There He bore our sins and our sorrows, the cost of our peace being laid upon Him, that by His stripes we might be healed. He gave His precious blood as "the blood of the everlasting covenant" that by it He might gain an entrance for us into the very presence of God. Now Christ is at the right hand of God as our High Priest, applying within our hearts, as a living Savior, the divine power of that propitiation. Whenever we think of drawing near to God, of serving Him, and of offering ourselves to Him, the thought is ever present: Can I in my sinfulness, with all my transgressions and shortcomings since my conversion, actually have fellowship with God every day? The answer is: We have been drawn close to God by the blood of Jesus. "Having . . . boldness by the blood of Jesus, let us draw near."

Have any of you felt afraid to make a complete surrender because you felt too unworthy? Consider this: Your worthiness is not in yourself or in the intensity or uprightness of your consecration; *your worthiness is in Christ Jesus.* We read in God's Word, it is "the altar that sanctifies the gift," and we know that Christ is not only the Priest and "the Lamb that was slain," but that the living Christ himself is the altar. Seven days the altar was to be sanctified by a sevenfold blood sprinkling; after that God said, "That altar shall be an altar most holy: whatever touches the altar shall be holy." And the New Testament teaches, "The altar sanctifies the gift." Christ is our altar. If anyone asks, "Can God accept me in my weakness?" Come, and do not be afraid. Lay yourself upon Christ, the living altar, the everlasting propitiation, who alone can make you acceptable to God every moment, and rest there. Rest upon Him in total repose and faith. Unworthy though I am, the altar sanctifies the gift; in Jesus, resting on Him, God accepts my frailty and I am well-pleasing in His sight. Seek to maintain this truth, not only as a doctrine for the comfort and salvation of the unconverted, declaring full and immediate pardon, but seek to maintain it as the power of continual access to God. "If we walk in the light as He is in the light, the blood of Jesus Christ his Son cleanses us from all sin." It is in Christ that the door to the heart of my Father is open at all times; it is through the blood of the blessed Lamb of God that the inflow of the divine life is available to your heart and mine.

Third, I not only have Christ before me as my example and Christ for me as my propitiation, but I have *Christ with me as my Savior from sin, my friend, my leader, and my guide.* Yes, that was the precious promise of our gracious Lord before He left: "And surely I am with you always." Earlier He had said, when the disciples did not yet understand Him, "Where two or three are gathered together in my name, there am I in the midst of them."

What you and I need to realize is that Jesus Christ is nearer to us than our closest earthly friend. If only we took the time to turn our eyes and hearts away from this world, even from the faces of family and friends that surround us, the joys that attract us and distract us, and fix them steadfastly on the face of Jesus, He would manifest himself to our hearts and we would be filled with the consciousness that He is with us. You know how deep is the consciousness of a parent every morning as he rises, that he has beloved children who eagerly wake to be greeted and held and loved. It is so natural; the whole heart is so full of it that it does not need a conscious thought. Can it be that Christ can make His presence as near and as clear and as dear to me as the fellowship of the ones dearest to me on earth? Christ can do it and longs to do it and is worthy that we should allow Him to do it. *O God, when will the time come when your Son will be nearer to us than father or mother, wife or husband, child or brother? May that blessed hour come!*

Jesus Christ wants to live and walk with you that He may do this blessed work in you. He wants to be with you as your companion so that you will never be alone. There is no trial or difficulty through which you will have to pass without the promise of Jehovah—"I will be with you"—being fulfilled. No battle you have to fight with sin or temptation, no weakness that makes you tremble at the consciousness of what you are in yourself, but it is possible to have Christ at your side every moment. Jesus Christ is your leader, to show you the way you should walk; He is your companion, to comfort you by His presence and make your heart glad; He is your Savior from sin, in His mighty power watching over you and working in you all of God's good pleasure. Oh, that God might show us that the life of absolute surrender is a life that can be lived in Christ Jesus, a life that can be lived because Christ himself will care for us and watch over us.

And one final thought: *Christ in us is our life and our strength.* This is the crown of all. New believers usually understand very little of this. Many have had some experience of Christ with them as guide and helper, but have not come to realize what Christ in me as my very life and strength means. And yet that is what the apostle Paul tells us is the great gospel mystery, the mystery that was hid for generations but has now been revealed, the mystery of God's people, of which he says, "the riches of the glory of this mystery, which is Christ in you." Believers, the riches and glory of our God are manifest to you in this: God wants you to have Christ His Son living in you. May we come, then, not asking for a small blessing or a beginning of blessings, but to have our whole life opened up to the indwelling, controlling, sanctifying power of Jesus Christ.

I would like to address Christian workers. Our great thought has been that of *work*. But what is needed if God is to bless His workers? How is God's power to come and to work? Beloved, Christ is the power of God, and we need more of Christ, we need the whole Christ, we need Christ revealed in us by the Holy Spirit; then the power of God will work.

We referred to a church so filled with the Holy Spirit that He could say to that church, "Set apart for me the men that I have called for my work." We spoke of workers as people who are ready and willing to be set apart for the Holy Spirit. How can each church be brought to this condition? Only in one way. John the Baptist preached Christ who baptized "with the Holy Spirit and with fire." That tells me Jesus Christ is the one from whom the Holy Spirit must come in ever new and larger measure; if you want the power of God's Spirit to be revealed in and through the church, it must come from a closer attachment to Christ, a closer union with Him, a larger revelation of Christ dwelling in believers. A blessing then must come. Did not Jesus say, "He that believes in me, out of him shall flow rivers of living water"? And is not this by faith, *by believing that Christ comes and dwells in the heart* and becomes the fountain out of which the Holy Spirit flows? What do we read in the last chapter of the Revelation of John? "And He showed me a pure river of water of life, clear as crystal, proceeding out of the throne of God and of the Lamb." Yes, when the Lamb sat down upon the throne of glory, the river of water of life flowed out. It is the Lamb who must lead us to the fountains of living water and give them within our hearts, so that we will have power to work among men—not the power of reason, not the power of human love, zeal, earnestness, and diligence, but the power that comes from God.

Are you ready for that power? Are you ready to surrender yourself absolutely to God and receive it? Can you truly say, "Lord, I am totally surrendered to you. It is done in weakness and in trembling, but it is done. I have received a small portion of what I know you can give, but as an empty vessel, cleansed and humble, I place myself at your feet again, day by day and moment by moment, and I wait upon you"? And, believer, what no eye has

Chapter 9

We Can Remain in His Love At All Times

The fruit of the Spirit is love.

Galatians 5:22

It is easy to understand why I chose this subject. We have addressed the great need for believers to be brought together and united in one spirit and one body. We said that one of the great reasons why God cannot bless is *the lack of love* in the church. When the body is divided, strength is diminished.

Only when believers stand as one body, one before God in the fellowship of love, one toward another in deep affection, one before the world in a love that the world can see—only then will they have power to secure the blessing they ask from God. Remember, a vessel that is cracked or broken into many pieces cannot be filled. You can take a piece of a broken vessel and dip out a little water with it, but if you want the vessel to be full and useful, it must be whole. That is literally true of Christ's church, and if there is one thing we still must pray for it is this: "Lord melt us together into one by the power of the Holy Spirit; let the

Holy Spirit, who at Pentecost made them all one heart and one soul, do His blessed work among us." Praise God, we can love each other in a divine love, for "the fruit of the Spirit is love." Yield yourselves to love and the Holy Spirit will come; receive the Spirit and He will teach you to love more.

The reason, of course, that the fruit of the Spirit is love is because God is love. And what does that mean? It is the very nature and being of God to delight in communicating himself. God knows nothing of selfishness. He keeps nothing to himself. *God's nature is to be always giving.* In the sun, the moon, and the stars, in every flower you see it, in every bird of the air, every fish of the sea. God communicates life to His creatures. Even the angels around His throne, the seraphim and cherubim, who are flames of fire, receive their brightness and their glory from the presence of God. And God delights to pour out His love on us— His redeemed children. From eternity God had His only begotten Son. The Father gave Him all things, and nothing that God had was held back. God is love.

One of the old church Fathers said that the best way to understand the Trinity was through the revelation of divine love—the Father, the loving one, the Fountain of Love; the Son, the beloved one, the Reservoir of Love in whom the love was poured out; and the Spirit, the living love that united both and then overflowed into this world. The Spirit of Pentecost, the Spirit of the Father and the Spirit of the Son, is love. When the Holy Spirit comes to us and to others, will He be less a Spirit of love than He is in God? It cannot be; He cannot change His nature. The Spirit of God is love, and the fruit of the Spirit is love.

Love has always been the one great need of mankind; it was the thing that Christ's redemption came to accomplish: *to restore love to this world*. When man sinned, selfishness triumphed—he sought self instead of God. Adam at once accused the woman of having led him astray. Love to God had gone, love to man was lost. Of the first two children of Adam, one became a murderer of his brother. Does that not teach us that sin had robbed the world of love? The history of the world has been of love lost! The Lord Jesus Christ came from heaven as the Son of God's love. "God so loved the world that he gave his only begotten Son." God's Son demonstrated what love is. He lived a life of love on earth in fellowship with His disciples, in compassion for the poor and miserable, in love even to His enemies, and He died the death of love. And when He went to heaven, He sent down the Spirit of love to banish selfishness and envy and pride, and bring the love of God into the hearts of men. The fruit of the Spirit is love.

And what was the preparation for the promise of the Holy Spirit? That promise is found in John 16. But remember what precedes it in the thirteenth chapter. Before Christ promised the Holy Spirit, He gave a new commandment and said wonderful things about it. One thing was, "Even as I have loved you, so you must love one another." To them His dying love was to be the only law of their conduct and interaction with each other. What a message to those fishermen, to those men full of pride and selfishness! "Learn to love each other," said Christ, "as I have loved you." And by the grace of God they did it. When Pentecost came they were of one heart and one soul. Christ did it for them.

And then He said, "By this shall all men know that you are my disciples, if you have love for one another." You all know what it is to wear a badge. Christ said to His disciples, in effect: "I give you a badge, and that badge is *love*; that is to be your mark. It is *the only thing* in heaven or on earth by which men can know me."

Should we not fear that *love has fled from the earth?* If we were to ask the world if it has seen us wear the badge of *love,* what would its answer be? As the world views the church of Christ, can it find a place where there is no quarrelling and separation? Let us ask God with one heart that we may wear the badge of *love.* God is able to give it.

Nothing but love can expel and conquer our selfishness. Self is the great curse, whether in its relation to God or toward others—thinking only of ourselves and seeking our own. Self is our greatest curse. But, praise God, Christ came to redeem us from self. We sometimes talk about deliverance from the self-life, and we should praise God for every word that can be said to help us. But I am afraid some people think deliverance from the self-life means that they will have no more troubles serving God. And they forget that *deliverance from the self-life means to be a vessel overflowing with love to everyone every day.*

Here we have the reason why so many people pray for the power of the Holy Spirit and yet receive so little of it. They pray for power for their work and for blessing, but they have not prayed for power for full deliverance from self. That means not only the righteous self in relationship with God but also the unloving self in relationship with men. But there is deliverance. "The fruit of the Spirit is love." I bring you the glorious promise that Christ is able to fill our hearts with love.

Many of us try hard to love. We even force ourselves to love. Not that it is entirely wrong—perhaps it is better than nothing. But the result is usually sad. Continual failure is its fruit. The reason is simply this: Our own efforts at love are not the same as having the Holy Spirit pour out God's love into our hearts. How often we have limited the text "The love of God is shed abroad in our hearts." It is often understood in the sense that it means the love of God *to me.* But what a limitation! That is only the beginning. It means the love of God in its entirety, in its fullness as an indwelling power, a love of God to me that leaps back to Him in love, and overflows to others in love—God's love to me, my love to God, and my love to others. The three are one; you cannot separate them. Believe that the love of God can remain in us at all times.

How little we have understood this. Why is a lamb always gentle? Because it is its very nature to be gentle. Does it cost the lamb any trouble or effort to be gentle? Does a lamb study to be gentle? Why does it come so easy? It is its nature. Likewise, it is the nature of a wolf to trouble the sheep. Because that is its nature. It does not have to summon up its courage; it is inherent.

So how can I learn to love? I cannot really learn or know it until the Spirit of God fills my heart with God's love and I begin to long for His love in a very different sense from which I have sought it so selfishly: as comfort and joy, happiness or pleasure to myself. I cannot until I begin to learn that "God is love," and claim and receive it as an indwelling power for self-sacrifice. I cannot until I begin to see that my glory, my blessedness, is to be like God and like Christ in yielding everything in myself for others. May God teach us that! Oh, the divine blessedness of the love with which the Holy Spirit can fill our hearts! "The fruit of the Spirit is love."

When we speak about the consecrated life, we often speak about *disposition,* and some have said too much is made of it. I, personally, do not think we can make too much of it. Disposition is a mirror of whether the love of Christ is filling the heart. Many find it easier in the church or in a prayer meeting to be holy and happy than in the daily life with their families and co-workers—easier to be holy and happy outside the home than in it. Where is the love of God? In Christ. God has prepared a wonderful redemption in Christ and part of it is to make something supernatural of us. Have we learned to desire it, to ask for it, and to expect it in its fullness?

Then there is the *tongue*! Just think what liberty many believers give to their tongues. They say, "I have a right to think and say what I like." When they speak about each other, when they speak about their neighbors, when they speak about other believers, how often sharp remarks are used! God keep me from saying anything that would be unloving; God shut my mouth if I am not speaking in tender love. But what I am saying is true. How often though believers are banded together in work, they are still full of sharp criticism, rash judgment, hasty opinions, unloving words, secret contempt for each other, and hidden condemnation of others. Just as a mother's love covers her children, delights in them, and has the tenderest compassion for them despite their failures, so there should be in the heart of every believer such an unconditional love toward every brother and sister in Christ. Have you aimed for it? Sought it? Pleaded for it? Jesus Christ said, "As I have loved you . . . love one another." He did not place it among the other commandments, but He said in effect, "This is a new commandment: Love one another as I have loved you."

What is the reason that the Holy Spirit cannot come in power? Remember the comparison I used in speaking of the vessel. I can dip a broken piece of the vessel into water, but if a vessel is to be full it must be unbroken. Wherever believers come together, to whatever church or mission or ministry they belong, they must love one another intensely or the Spirit of God cannot do His work. We talk about grieving the Spirit of God by worldliness, ritualism, formality, error, and indifference, but I believe the greatest thing that grieves God's Spirit is a lack of love among His children. Let us ask God to search our hearts regarding a love like His.

Why are we taught that the fruit of the Spirit is love? Because the Spirit of God has come to make our daily life a demonstration of divine power and a revelation of what God can do for His children. Think of the church at large. What divisions! Think of the different denominations. Take the question of holiness, of the cleansing blood, of the baptism of the Spirit—what differences are caused among dear believers by such questions! That there should be differences of opinion does not trouble me. But how often hate, bitterness, contempt, separation, and unloving action have surrounded the holiest truths of God's Word! It was so in the time of the Reformation between the Lutheran and Calvinistic churches. What bitterness there was then in regard to the Lord's Supper, which was meant to be the bond of union between all believers! And so, down through the ages, the very dearest truths of God have become mountains that have separated us. If we want to pray in power, if we desire the Holy Spirit to come down in power and to be poured out, we must covenant with God that we will love one another with a heavenly love. Are you ready for it? Only true love is large enough to take in all God's children, even the most unloving, unlovable, unworthy, unbearable and trying. If our absolute surrender to God was genuine, then it must mean absolute surrender to the divine love to fill us; to be a servant of love is to love every child of God around us.

God did something wonderful when He gave the glorified Christ the Holy Spirit to be sent down from the heart of the

Father to His children. Let us not degrade the Holy Spirit into a mere power by which we carry on our work! God forgive us. Oh, that the Holy Spirit might be held in honor as a person of the Trinity and as a power to fill us with the very life and nature of the Father and of Christ!

We need love to bind us to each other as well as a divine love in our work for the lost around us. Do we not often undertake a great deal of work just as men undertake the work of philanthropy, from a natural spirit of compassion for others? Do we not often undertake Christian work because our minister or friend asks us to, or because we see the need and respond out of duty or obligation and yet without having had a baptism of love?

People often ask, "What is the baptism of fire?" I have answered that I know no fire like the fire of God, the fire of everlasting love that consumed the sacrifice on Calvary. The baptism of love is what the church needs; to receive it we must begin at once to get down upon our faces before God in confession and plead, "Lord, let love from heaven flow down into my heart. I am yielding my life to pray and live as one who has surrendered himself so that the everlasting love can dwell in me and fill me." Yes, if the love of God were in our hearts, what a difference it would make! There are many who say, "I work for Christ, and I feel I could work much more, but I do not have the gift; I do not know how or where to begin, I do not know what I can do." Brother, sister, ask God to baptize you with the Spirit of love, and love will find its way. Love is a fire that will burn through every difficulty. God fill us with love!

Without love we cannot do our work. May God baptize our ministers, our missionaries, our evangelists, our Sunday school teachers, and our young people with compassionate love.

It is only love that can enable us for the work of intercession. I have said before that love must enable us for our work. And do you know what is the hardest and yet the most important work? It is the work of intercession, the work of going to God and taking time to lay hold on Him. A man may be a diligent believer, an eager pastor, a faithful follower, but how often must he confess that he knows very little of what it is to wait upon God! May God give us that great gift of an intercessory spirit, a spirit of prayer and supplication! Let me ask you to make it a habit . . . not to let another day pass without praying for God's people.

I find there are believers who think little of true intercession. I find prayer meetings where they pray for their own members, for their own trials and troubles, but barely reach beyond their own small group, let alone the world. Take time to pray for the church citywide, nationwide, and worldwide. It is only right to pray for the lost as I have already said. God help us to pray more for them. It is right to pray for missionaries and for evangelistic work, for the heathen or the unconverted. Paul did say to pray for believers. The condition of Christ's church is indescribably lacking. Plead for God's people that He would visit them, plead for each other, and for all believers who are trying to work for God. Let love fill your heart. Ask Christ to pour love into you every day. Receive the Holy Spirit's instruction: *I am set apart to the Holy Spirit, and the fruit of the Spirit is love.* God help us to understand it.

We have often mentioned the place of waiting upon God. May God grant that we learn day by day to wait more expectantly upon Him. If you wait upon God only for yourself, the power to do so will soon be lost; but give yourself to the ministry and the love of intercession, and pray more for God's people around you, for the

— *Chapter 10*—

What Is Impossible With Men Is Possible With God

Jesus replied, "What is impossible with men is possible with God."

Luke 18:27

Christ told the rich young ruler, "Sell everything you have and give to the poor, and you will have treasure in heaven. Then come, follow me" (v. 22). The young man became very sad when he heard this. Christ turned to the disciples and said, "How hard it is for the rich to enter the kingdom of God!" The disciples, we read, were greatly astonished and answered, "If it is so difficult to enter the kingdom, who then can be saved?" And Christ gave this positive answer: "What is impossible with men is possible with God."

By now we have prayed and listened to God's Word with renewed encouragement. What can we say to encourage each other to follow through on what God has spoken? I trust that this word will be full of faith and confidence, that the Holy Spirit will breathe it into our hearts, and that we shall go on with one thought: "What is impossible with men is possible with God." May God help us to open our ears and hearts to the blessed Lord Jesus until He speaks this truth into the very depths of our being.

The text contains two thoughts: (1) *Concerning salvation and following Christ by a holy life: It is impossible for men to do it on their own.* (2) *What is impossible with men is possible with God.* Let us look at these two sides.

The two thoughts mark the two great lessons that man has to learn in the spiritual life. It often takes a long time to learn the first lesson, that spiritually man can do nothing, that salvation is impossible to him alone. And often if a man learns that, he does not learn the second lesson: What has been impossible to me is possible with God. Blessed is the man who learns both lessons.

Learning these two lessons characterizes two stages in the Christian's life. The initial stage sees a man trying to do his utmost and failing, then trying to do still better and failing again, then trying still more and always failing. Unfortunately, he very often still does not learn the lesson: *It is impossible.* Peter spent three years in Christ's school and never learned that word *impossible* until he denied his Lord and went out and wept bitterly. Then he learned the lesson: *With man it is impossible to serve God.*

Just look for a moment at a man who is learning this lesson: *It is impossible with man.* At first he fights against it; then he submits to it, but reluctantly and in despair; at last he accepts it willingly and rejoices in it. At the beginning of the Christian life the new believer has no understanding of this truth. He has been converted, he has the joy of the Lord in his heart, he begins to run the race and fight the battle; he is sure he can conquer because he is sincere and honest and God will help him. Yet, somehow, very soon he fails where he did not expect it and sin gets the better of him. He is disappointed, but he thinks: *I was not watchful enough, I did not make my commitments strong enough.* So again he vows, again he prays, and yet he fails. He thinks: *Am I not born again? Have I not the life of God within me?* And he thinks again: *Yes, and I have Christ to help me. I can live the holy life.*

Later he comes to another stage. He sees that such a life is impossible, but he does not accept it. There are multitudes of believers who come to this point: "I cannot do it, therefore God never expected me to do what I cannot do." If you tell them that God does expect it, it appears to them a mystery. Many live a life of failure and sin instead of rest and victory because they begin to see: "I cannot; it is impossible." And yet they do not understand it fully, and so under the impression *I cannot,* they give way to thoughts of despair. They will do their best, but they never expect to be successful.

But God leads His children on to a third stage. This is when a man receives the word *It is impossible* in its full strength, and yet at the same time says, "I must do it and I will do it—it is impossible for man, and yet I must do it"; when the renewed will begins to exercise its whole power, and in intense longing and prayer begins to cry to God, "Lord, what does this mean—how am I to be freed from the power of sin?" It is the state of the regenerate man in Romans 7. There you find the believer trying his utmost to live a holy life. God's law has been revealed to him as reaching down into the very depth of the desires of the heart, and the man dares to say, "I delight in the law of God after the inward man. To will what is good is present with me. My heart loves the law of God and my will has chosen that law." Can a man like that fail, with his heart full of delight in God's law and with his will determined to do what is right? Yes. That is what Romans 7 teaches.

There is something lacking. Not only must I delight in the law of God after the inward man and will what God wills, but I need divine omnipotence to work it in me. That is what the apostle Paul teaches in Philippians 2:13: "It is God who works in you to will and to act."

Note the contrast. In Romans 7:18 the regenerate man says, "For I have the desire to do what is good, but I cannot carry it out." But in Philippians 2 you have a man who has been led further, a man who understands that when God has worked the renewed will, He will give the power to accomplish what that will desires. Let us receive this as the first great lesson in the spiritual life: It is impossible for me; let there be an end of the flesh and all its powers, an end of self, and let it be my joy to be helpless. Praise God for the divine teaching that makes us helpless!

In *absolute surrender to God* we are meant to be brought to an end of ourselves and yet we may feel: "I cannot see how I can actually live as absolutely surrendered to God every moment—in my home, in my business, in the midst of trials and temptations." Here we need to learn the lesson: If you feel you cannot do it, you are on the right road. Accept that position and maintain it before God: "My heart's desire, O God, is to be absolutely surrendered to you, but I cannot perform it. It is impossible for me to live this life; it is beyond me." Fall before Him and learn that when you are utterly helpless, God will come in and be all you need.

The second lesson: "What is impossible with men *is possible with God.*" Many only learn *It is impossible with men,* and then give up in helpless despair and live a wretched Christian life without joy, or strength, or victory. Why? Because they do not humble themselves to learn the rest of it: *With God all things are possible.*

Your daily spiritual life is proof that God works impossibilities;

your spiritual life is to be a series of impossibilities made possible and actual by God's almighty power. That is what the Christian needs. He has an almighty God whom he worships, and he must understand: I do not want a little of God's power, but I want—with reverence it is said—the whole of God's omnipotence to keep me and to enable me to live like Christ.

The whole of Christianity is a work of God's omnipotence. Look at the birth of Christ. The miracle of divine power was announced to Mary: "With God nothing shall be impossible." It was the omnipotence of God. Look at Christ's resurrection. We are told that it was according to *the exceeding greatness of His almighty power* that God raised Christ from the dead.

Every tree must grow on the root from which it springs. An oak tree three hundred years old grows on the same root from which it had its beginning. Christianity had its beginning in the omnipotence of God, and in every soul it must have its continuance in that same power. All the possibilities for spiritual growth have their origin in a new apprehension of Christ's power to work all God's will in us. I want to call you to come and worship an almighty God. Have you learned to do it? Have you learned to deal so closely with the almighty God that you know His power works in you? Outwardly there may be little sign of it. The apostle Paul said, "I came to you in weakness and fear, and with much trembling. My message and my preaching were not with wise and persuasive words, but with a demonstration of the Spirit's power" (1 Corinthians 2:3–4). From the human side there was weakness; from the divine side there was omnipotence. That is true of every godly life. If we would only learn that lesson better and give a wholehearted, undivided surrender to it, we would know the blessing of dwelling every hour and every moment with the almighty God.

Have you ever studied the attribute of God's omnipotence? You know that it was God's omnipotence that created the world, light out of darkness, and man. But have you studied God's omnipotence in the works of redemption?

Look at Abraham. When God called him to be the father of that people from which Christ was to be born, God said to him, "I am the Almighty God; walk before me and be perfect." God trained Abraham to trust Him as the Omnipotent One. We see it in his departure to a land that he knew not and in his faith as a pilgrim living among the Canaanites—his faith that said, "This is my land." We see it in his faith in waiting twenty-five years for a son in his old age, against all hope. Abraham even believed God for the raising up of Isaac from the dead on Mount Moriah when he was told to sacrifice him. He was strong in faith, giving glory to God, because he accounted Him who had promised able to perform.

The reason for the weakness of your Christian life is that you try to work it out on your own, only allowing God to help you when you are desperate. This cannot be. You must become utterly helpless, allowing God to work in you and through you and for you unreservedly. This is what we need if we are truly to be servants of God. I could trace through Scripture and show how Moses, when he led Israel out of Egypt; how Joshua, when he brought them into the land of Canaan; how all God's servants in the Old Testament counted upon the omnipotence of God to do the impossible. And this same God lives and is ours today. Yet some of us still want God to give us a little help while we do our best, instead of understanding that God wants us to say, "I can do nothing; God must do all." Have you said, "In worship, in work, in sanctification, in obedience to God, I can do nothing of myself; my place is to worship the omnipotent God and to believe that He will work in me every moment"? May God teach you. May God by His grace show you what He is like, so worthy of your trust—an omnipotent God, willing, with His full power to place himself at the disposal of every believer. Shall we not believe the lesson of the Lord Jesus and say, "Amen; the things which are impossible with men are possible with God"?

Apply this lesson to what we have said in previous chapters. We said that the church must be a place so set apart to the Holy Spirit that it has power to set apart men. And every worker is to be set apart to the Holy Spirit. That is clearly established from God's Word. But has your heart really been expecting that God will make this true? Do you believe it possible that the everlasting God can say by the Holy Spirit that all the workers in your church are set apart to the Holy Spirit and they live day by day like men and women set apart, not for this or that ministry, but set apart to the Holy Spirit? Can we expect in the church of Christ that this life will be a reality? "What is impossible with men is possible with God." If we fall on our faces before God and say, "It is impossible . . ." God will honor our faith.

Remember what we said about Peter—his self-confidence, self-power, self-will, and how he came to deny his Lord. You may have felt: "There is the self-life; there is the flesh-life that rules in me!" Now, have you believed that there is deliverance from that? Have you believed that the Almighty God is able to so reveal Christ in your heart, to so call on the Holy Spirit to rule in you, that the self-life shall not have power or dominion over you? Have you coupled the two together and with tears of repentance and deep humility cried out, "O God, it is impossible for me; I cannot do it, but, glory to your name, it is possible with God"? Have you claimed deliverance? Come, and do it now. Newly surrender yourself into the hands of a God of infinite love; and as infinite as His love is so is His power to do it.

We also spoke of absolute surrender, and felt that this is the great lack in the church of Christ, this is why the Holy Spirit cannot fill us, and this is why we cannot live as people entirely set apart to the Holy Spirit. Is it any wonder that the flesh and the self-life cannot be conquered? We have never understood what it is to be absolutely surrendered to God as Jesus was. I know many earnest and honest believers who say, "Amen. I accept the message of absolute surrender to God; and yet I tremble and wonder, *Will that ever be mine? Can I count upon God to make me one of whom it shall be said in heaven, on earth, and in hell: He lives in absolute surrender to God?* Believe that when He takes charge of you in Christ, it is possible for God to make you a man or woman of absolute surrender. And God is able to maintain that. He can enable you to rise from your bed every morning with the blessed thought directly or indirectly: *I am in God's charge; my God is working out my life for me.*

Some of you are weary of thinking about sanctification. You pray, you long and cry for it, and yet it appears so far off! The holiness and humility of Jesus seems so distant. Beloved friends, the one doctrine of sanctification that is scriptural and real and effectual is our recurring truth: What is impossible with men is possible with God. God can sanctify us, and by His almighty power, He can keep us too. May the light of God shine on you and may you know your God better by the time you have finished this chapter.

It is only God by His Spirit who can reveal the life of Christ in us—what it is to live like Christ and to experience Him as our Savior from sin and our daily strength. The apostle Paul said that He would grant us according to the riches of His glory to be strengthened with might by His Spirit in the inner man. This is the omnipotence of God working in the hearts of His believing children. You may have tried to grasp it, to believe it, but to no avail. It is because you have not fully grasped the truth that the things impossible with men are possible with God.

When we have the inflowing of the love of God from above, from the fountain of everlasting love, it will be as natural for me to love others as it is natural for the lamb to be gentle and the wolf to be its predator. This is the heart condition where the more someone hates or speaks evil of me, the more unlikable and unlovable he is, the more I will love him; the more obstacles and hatred and ingratitude, the more the power of love triumphs in me. This condition can never be mine until I am able to say, "It is impossible with men." But if I have been led to say, "This message has spoken to me about a love utterly beyond my power; it is absolutely impossible," then we can come to God and say, "It is possible with God."

Why do I speak so specifically regarding your spiritual life? For this one reason: A man or a woman who is to work with power for others must know the power of God in his or her own soul. Let every believer's heart cry out with the earnest prayer: *Lord, may your Spirit rest upon me and never depart from me. Prove your mighty power in my soul day by day, in such a way that all men will see that God is almighty to save and to keep.*

We desire that our lives count for God. Dear friends, labor with a joyous face, with a heart full of hope and buoyant expectancy. Cry to God for a great revival. It is the unceasing prayer of my heart that God would revive His believing people. When I think of all the unconverted in the church, the skeptics, the wayward, and the perishing around me, my heart cries out, "My God, revive your church and your people!" However weak some believers may be, if they are children of God, they are your brothers and sisters. We must, then, pray for them, helping them out of darkness and out of the prison in which they find themselves. It is not without reason that there is within your heart yearnings after holiness and consecration. It is a forerunner of God's power. Our omnipotent God will do in us more than we can ask. Paul ascribed glory to Him who is able to do exceeding abundantly above all that we ask or think. Let our hearts agree.

Come together with new consecration, new hope, new courage, and new joy. Believe that God Almighty is with you. Let it be as it was in Israel: "Behold, this is our God; we have waited for him, and he will save us; this is the Lord, we have waited for him; we will be glad and rejoice in his salvation."

Surrounding you is a world of sin and sorrow, and the devil is present in it. Remember, Christ is on the throne; Christ is stronger. He has conquered and will conquer. Go about your work more humble, broken, and dependent on Him than ever before. Praise God that He can work this attitude in every one of us if we but wait on Him. Our text declares that all things are *impossible with men*, but the contrast is that all things are *possible with God*. Join together with God. Adore Him and trust Him as the only One for your own life as well as for all those souls that are entrusted to you. Like Abraham, you will become strong in faith, giving glory to God, because you account Him who promised able to perform it.

Chapter 11

What a Wretched Man I Am!

What a wretched man I am! Who will rescue me
from this body of death? Thanks be to God—
through Jesus Christ our Lord!

Romans 7:24–25

Perhaps you realize the wonderful place this text has in the epistle to the Romans. It stands at the end of the seventh chapter as the gateway to the eighth. In the first sixteen verses of the eighth chapter, the Holy Spirit is mentioned sixteen times; you have there the description and promise of the life that a child of God can live in the power of the Holy Spirit. This begins in the second verse: "Through Christ Jesus the law of the Spirit of life set me free from the law of sin and death." From there Paul goes on to speak of the great privileges of the believer who is led by the Spirit of God. The gateway into all of this is in verse 24 of chapter 7: "What a wretched man I am!" They are the words of a man who has come to the end of himself. In the previous verses he describes how he has struggled in his own power to obey the law of God and failed.

But in answer to his own question of who will rescue him from this body of death, he now finds the true answer and cries, "Thanks be to God—through Jesus Christ our Lord!" From there he goes on to describe the deliverance that he has found.

From these words I want to describe the path by which a man can be led out of the spirit of bondage and into the spirit of liberty. We know it has been said, "You did not receive a spirit that makes you a slave again to fear" (Romans 8:15). We are continually warned that the great danger of the Christian life is to return to our former life of bondage. I want to describe the man who escapes bondage and finds liberty.

First, these words are the language of a *regenerate* man; second, of a *helpless* man; third, of a *wretched* man, and fourth, of a man *on the border of complete liberty.*

In the first place, then, are *the words of a regenerate man.* This is clearly in evidence from verse 17 of chapter 7: "It is no longer I myself who do it, but it is sin living in me." That is the language of a regenerate man, a man who knows that his heart and nature have been renewed and that sin is now a power in him that is not of himself. "For in my inner being I delight in God's law." Again, this is the language of a regenerate man. He dares to say when he does what is evil: "It is no longer I myself who do it, but it is sin living in me." It is important to understand this.

In the first two great sections of the epistle, Paul deals with justification and sanctification. In dealing with justification, he lays the foundation of the doctrine in the teaching about sin—not in the singular but in the plural: "sins." These represent actual transgressions. In the second part of the fifth chapter he begins to deal with sin, not as actual transgression, but as a power. Imagine what a loss it would have been if we did not have the second half of chapter 7. We would have missed the question we all want answered! And what is the answer? The regenerate man is one in whom the will has been renewed and who can say, "I delight in God's law."

Second, *the regenerate man is also a helpless man.* Here is the mistake made by many believers. They think that a renewed will is enough, but that is not the case. This regenerate man tells us, "I have the desire to do what is good, but I cannot carry it out." How often people say, "You have a new will, and if you determine to obey, you can do whatever you wish." But this man was as determined as anyone and yet made the confession that he could not carry out his good desires.

But, you ask, "Why does God make a regenerate man utter such a confession, when he has a willing heart and longs to do his utmost to love God?" And I ask, Why has God given us a will? Did the angels who fell have the strength to stand in their own will? The will of the creature is nothing but an empty vessel in which the power of God is to be made manifest. The creature is meant to find in God all that it is to be. You have it in the second chapter of the epistle to the Philippians, and you have it here also, that God's work is to work in us both to *will* and to *do* of His good pleasure. Here is a man who appears to say, "God has not worked the *doing* in me." How is the apparent contradiction to be reconciled?

You will find that in this passage (7:6–25) the Holy Spirit is not mentioned. The man is wrestling and struggling on his own to fulfill God's law. In contrast, the law is mentioned nearly twenty times. It describes a believer doing his very best to obey the law of God with his regenerate will. Not only this, but you will find the little words *I, me,* and *my* occur more than forty times. It is the regenerate "I" in its helplessness seeking to obey the law without being filled with the Spirit. This experience is common to nearly every believer. After conversion a man begins to do his best and fails; but if we are brought into the full light, we need fail no longer. Nor need we fail at all if we have received the Spirit in His fullness at conversion.

God allows failure so that the regenerate man understands his own utter lack of power. It is in the course of this struggle that there comes to us a sense of our utter sinfulness. It is God's way of dealing with us. He allows a man to strive to fulfill the law so that as he strives and wrestles, he may be brought to admit: "I am a regenerate child of God, but I am utterly helpless to obey His law." Notice the strong words used throughout the chapter to describe this condition: "I am unspiritual, sold as a slave to sin. I see another law at work in the members of my body, waging war against the law of my mind and making me a prisoner of the law of sin at work within my members." And last of all, "What a wretched man I am! Who will rescue me from this body of death?" The believer who bows here in deep contrition is utterly unable to obey the law of God.

Third, *not only is the man who makes this confession a regenerate but a powerless man, he is also a wretched man.* He is utterly unhappy and miserable. What is it that makes him so utterly miserable? It is because He loves God deeply, but he feels he is not obeying God. He says with brokenness of heart: "I do not understand what I do. For what I want to do I do not do, but what I hate I do. And if I do what I do not want to do, I agree that the law is good. As it is, it is no longer I myself who do it, but it is sin living in me." Blessed be God when a man learns to say, "What a wretched man I am!" from the depth of his heart. He is on the way to the eighth chapter of Romans.

Many make this confession a pillow for sin. If Paul had to confess his weakness and helplessness in this way, who am I that I should expect to do better? So the call to holiness is quietly set aside. But each of us must learn to say these words in the very spirit in which they are written here. When we hear sin spoken of as the abominable thing that God hates, do we take it lightly? All Christians who go on sinning without thought should take this verse to heart. Whenever you utter an unkind word, say, "What a wretched man I am!" And every time you lose your temper, kneel before God and realize that God never intended that you remain in this condition. We must take this word into our daily lives and repeat it every time we defend our own honor, say unkind words, or sin against the Lord God. May we be reminded of the Lord Jesus Christ in His humility, in His obedience, and in His self-sacrifice. When a man is brought to true confession of his miserable state, deliverance is at hand.

Remember, it was not only the sense of being powerless and held captive that made Paul know his wretchedness, but above all it was his sense of sinning against God. The law was doing its work, making sin *exceedingly sinful* in his sight. The thought of continually grieving God became utterly unbearable and brought out the painful cry of feeling wretched and undone. As long as we talk and reason about our failure and only try to discover the meaning of Romans 7, it will be of little benefit. But when *every sin* gives new intensity to our sense of wretchedness, when we feel our whole condition as one of not only helplessness but sinfulness, then we will be pressed not only to ask who will deliver us but to cry our thanks to God that it is through Jesus Christ our Lord.

Fourth, *when a man arrives at this point, he is on the very brink of deliverance.* The man has tried to obey the holy law of God. He has loved the law, he has wept over his sin, and he has tried to overcome it. He has tried to triumph over every fault, but every time his efforts have ended in failure. What did Paul mean by "the body of this death"? Did he mean his dying body? No. In the eighth chapter you have the answer: "The mind of sinful man is death." And "if you live according to the sinful nature, you will die; but if by the Spirit you put to death the misdeeds of the body, you will live." That is the body of death from which he is seeking deliverance. And now he is on the brink of deliverance! In chapter 7, verse 23, we have the words "But I see another law at work in the members of my body, waging war against the law of my mind and making me a prisoner of the law of sin at work within my members." It is *a captive* that cries: "Who will rescue me from this body of death?" He is a man who feels himself bound. But look to the contrast in verse 2 of chapter 8: "Through Christ Jesus the law of the Spirit of life set me free from the law of sin and death." That is the deliverance through Jesus Christ our Lord; the *liberty* the Spirit brings to the captive. Can you keep bound a man made free by the "law of the Spirit of life in Christ Jesus"?

But you say, "Didn't the regenerate man have the Spirit of Jesus when he spoke in the sixth chapter?"

Yes, *but he did not know what the Holy Spirit could do for him.* God does not work by His Spirit as a blind force in nature. He leads His people as reasonable, intelligent beings. Therefore, when He desires to give us the Holy Spirit whom He has promised, He shows us ourselves and the conviction that though we have been striving to obey the law, we have utterly failed. When we have come to that end, He shows us that in the Holy Spirit we have the power to obey, the power of victory, and the power of true holiness.

God works *to will* and He is ready to work *to do,* but many Christians misunderstand this. They think that because they have the will it is enough and they are able to do it. This is not so. The new will is a permanent gift, an attribute of the new nature. The power to do is not a permanent gift, but must be each moment received from the Holy Spirit. It is the man who is conscious *of his own powerlessness as a believer* who will learn that by the Holy Spirit *he can live a holy life.* This man is on the brink of a great deliverance; the way has been prepared for the glorious eighth chapter of Romans.

I come to you with a serious question: Where are you living? Are you saying you are wretched and looking for deliverance, with an occasional experience of the power of the Holy Spirit? Or are you thanking God through Jesus Christ for the law of the Spirit that has set you free from the law of sin and death?

What the Holy Spirit does is give the victory, if by the Spirit you mortify the deeds of the flesh. Again, it is the Holy Spirit who does this—the third person of the Godhead. He it is who, when the heart is opened to receive Him, comes in and reigns and puts to death the deeds of the body, day by day, hour by hour, and moment by moment.

I want to emphasize here that if these thoughts are to do us any good, they must bring us to a decision and to action. There are recorded in Scripture two very different types of believers. The Bible speaks in Romans, Corinthians, and Galatians about those who yield to the flesh; that is the life of tens of thousands of believers. Their lack of joy in the Holy Spirit and lack of the liberty He gives is owing to their walk in the flesh. The Spirit is within, but the flesh rules the life. To be led by the Spirit of God is what is sorely needed. You must begin to realize that God has given His Son Jesus Christ to watch over you every day, and your job is to trust. The work of the Holy Spirit is to enable you every moment to remember Jesus and to trust Him completely. The Spirit has come to keep the link with Him unbroken. Praise God for the Holy Spirit! We are so accustomed to thinking that the third person of the Trinity is a luxury, someone for special times or for special ministers with special talents. But the Holy Spirit is necessary for *every* believer, every moment of the day. Praise God that you have Him, and that He gives you the full experience of deliverance in Christ as He sets you free from the power of sin.

Do you long to have the power and the liberty of the Holy Spirit? Go before God in one final cry of despair: "O God, must I go on sinning forever? Who shall deliver me from myself, from this body of death?" Are you ready to sink before God and seek the power of Jesus to dwell in you and work in you? Are you ready to say, "I thank God through Jesus Christ"?

What good does it do to attend church services and seminars, to study our Bibles and pray, unless our lives are filled with the Holy Spirit? That is what God wants, and nothing else will enable you to live a life of power and peace. You know that when a parent asks his child a question, an answer is expected. How many believers are content with the question "Who shall deliver me from this body of death?" but never look for the answer. Instead of answering according to the Scriptures, they are silent. Instead of saying, "I thank God through Jesus Christ our Lord," they are forever repeating the question without the answer. If you want the path to full deliverance in Christ, to the liberty of the Spirit, and to the glorious liberty of the children of God, take it through the seventh chapter of Romans, and then say, "I thank God through Jesus Christ our Lord." Do not be content to remain ever groaning at your miserable state, but say, "Though I am a wretched man, I thank God through Jesus Christ. Even though I do not see it all, I am going to praise God." There is deliverance; there is the liberty of the Holy Spirit. The kingdom of God *is* "joy in the Holy Spirit."

—*Chapter 12*—

Having Begun
in the Spirit...

*I would like to learn just one thing from you: Did you receive
the Spirit by observing the law, or by believing what you heard?
Are you so foolish? After beginning with the Spirit, are you now
trying to attain your goal by human effort?*

Galatians 3:2–3

When we speak of the quickening, deepening, or strengthening of
the spiritual life, we are thinking of it in relationship to that which
is weak or wrong or sinful. It is a good thing to take our place
before God with the honest confession: "Dear God, my spiritual
life is not what it should be!"

As we look at the church as a whole we see so many indications of weakness, failure, sin, and shortcoming, that we are compelled to ask, How can this be? Is there any excuse for the church
of Christ to be living in such a low state? Or is it actually possible
that God's people should always be living in the joy and strength
of their God? Every believing heart must answer, "It *is* possible."

But again the questions arise: "Why is it, then, that God's

church as a whole is so powerless and the great majority of believers are not living up to their privileges? There must be a reason for it. Has God not given His Almighty Son to be the keeper of every believer, to make Christ an ever-present reality, and to impart and communicate to us all that we have in Christ? God has given His Son and His Spirit. Why is it that believers do not show this reality?"

We find in more than one of the epistles an answer to that question. In some of the epistles, such as 1 Thessalonians, Paul writes to the believers, in effect: "I want you to grow, to abound, to increase more and more." They were young, and although there were things lacking in their faith, their condition was satisfactory and gave him great joy. He writes time after time: I pray that you may abound more and more; I write to you to increase more and more. But there are other epistles where he takes a very different tone, especially the epistles to the Corinthians and the Galatians. He tells them in many different ways that the reason they were not living as believers are meant to live is that many of them were under the power of the flesh. My text is one example. He reminds them that by the preaching of faith they received the Holy Spirit. He had preached Christ to them; they had received Christ and had received the Holy Spirit in power. But what happened? Having begun in the Spirit, they tried to perfect the work that the Spirit had begun by their own fleshly effort. We find the same teaching in the epistles to the Corinthians.

This same solemn discovery is made in the church of Christ today. God has called the church to live in the power of the Holy Spirit, yet it is living for the most part in the power of human flesh, of will and energy and effort apart from the Spirit of God. I know this is the case with most believers. If God would permit me one message, it would be this: If the church will return to acknowledge that the Holy Spirit is her strength and her help, if it will return to surrender everything and wait upon God to be filled with the Spirit, her days of beauty and gladness will return and we shall see the glory of God revealed among us. This is my message to every individual believer: Nothing will help you unless you understand that you must live every day under the power of the Holy Spirit. God wants you to be a living vessel in whom the power of the Spirit is manifested every hour and every moment of your life, and God will enable you to be that.

Now let us turn our attention to what this word to the Galatians teaches us—some very simple thoughts. It shows us that *the beginning of the Christian life is receiving the Holy Spirit*. It shows us *the great danger of forgetting that we are to live by the Spirit* and not after the flesh. It shows us what *the fruits and the proofs are of our seeking perfection in the flesh*. And then it suggests to us *the way of deliverance from this condition*.

First of all, Paul says, "Having begun in the Spirit. . . ." Remember, the apostle not only preached justification by faith, but he preached something more. He preached—the epistle is full of it—that justified men can only live by the Holy Spirit and that God gives to every justified man the Holy Spirit to seal him. The apostle says to them more than once: "How did you receive the Holy Spirit? Was it by the preaching of the law or by the preaching of faith?" He could point back to that time when there had been a mighty revival under his teaching. The power of God had been manifested and the Galatians were compelled to confess: "Yes, we received the Holy Spirit—accepting Christ by faith, by faith we received the Holy Spirit."

Unfortunately, it is to be feared that many believers today

hardly understand that when they believed, they received the Holy Spirit. Many believers can say, "I received pardon and I received peace." But if you were to ask them, "Have you received the Holy Spirit?" they would hesitate; and some, if they were to say yes, would say it with hesitation. They would also tell you that since that time they have had little understanding of what it is to walk in the power of the Holy Spirit. Let us begin here and take hold of this great truth: The beginning of the true Christian life is to receive the Holy Spirit. This is the work of every Christian minister—as it was the work of Paul—to remind his people: Believers, you have already received the Holy Spirit and you must live according to His guidance and in His power.

If the Galatians who received the Holy Spirit in power were tempted to go astray by that awful danger of perfecting in the flesh what had been begun in the Spirit, how much more dangerous is it for believers today who barely understand that they have received the Holy Spirit, or who, if they know it as a matter of belief, seldom think of it and seldom praise God for it!

If we are sincerely asking what should be done to have Christ's church restored, we should begin by accepting the truth that the Holy Spirit must receive a far more honored position among us. In every believer there must be a deep, abiding conviction: What I received from God was not only pardon in heaven, but the Holy Spirit within my heart, to live there and to be my strength.

Second, having begun in the Spirit, *we must see the great danger of forgetting that we are to live by the Spirit.* You are familiar with railroad switches. A train may be running in a certain direction, but the switches at some place may not be properly opened or closed, and without notice the train is switched off to the right or to the left. If that takes place, the train speeds along in the wrong direction and may endanger the lives of all the people on board, whether they realize it or not.

Similarly, God gives the Holy Spirit with the intention that the believer's life would always be lived in the power of the Spirit. A man cannot live a godly life for one hour unless he is empowered by the Holy Spirit. He may live a respectable, consistent life, even an irreproachable life, a life of virtue and diligent service. But to live a life acceptable to God, in the enjoyment of God's salvation and God's love, to live and walk in the power of the new life he must be guided by the Holy Spirit every day and every hour.

But now hear the danger: The Galatians received the Holy Spirit, but what was begun in the Spirit they tried to perfect in the flesh. How? They fell back again under Judaizing teachers who told them they must be circumcised. They began to seek their religion in external observance. And so Paul uses the expression "they sought to glory in their flesh" concerning those teachers who wanted the Galatians circumcised. You sometimes hear the expression "religious flesh." What is meant by this? It is simply a phrase that expresses the thought that *human nature, human will,* and *human effort* can be very active in religion, even after one is converted and receives the Holy Spirit. I may begin in my own strength to try to serve God. I may be very diligent and doing a great deal, and yet all the time be doing the work by human strength rather than by God's Spirit. It is a solemn thought to think that man can, without noticing it, be switched from the "line" of the Holy Spirit onto the "line" of the flesh; that he can be working hard and making great sacrifices, and yet be doing all in the power of the human will! The great question for us to ask God in self-examination is that we may be shown whether our life is lived more in the power of the flesh than in the power of the

Holy Spirit. A man may be a good preacher, work energetically in his ministry, even be highly spoken of by others, and yet one can feel there is something lacking. You sense that he is not a spiritual man; there is little spirituality about his life. How many believers there are about whom no one would ever think of saying, "What a spiritual man he is!" This is the weakness of the church of Christ. It is all in the one word—*flesh*.

Now the flesh may manifest itself in many ways. It may be seen in fleshly wisdom. The mind may be very active about spiritual things. One may preach or write or think or meditate or delight in being occupied with things in the Scriptures and in God's kingdom, and yet the power of the Holy Spirit may be remarkably absent. I fear that if you were to evaluate the preaching throughout the church of Christ today and ask, "Why is there so little converting power in the preaching of the Word? Why is there so much effort and so little results for eternity? Why is it that the Word has so little power to build up believers in holiness and consecration?" The answer will be: It is the absence of the power of the Holy Spirit. There can be no other reason but that the flesh and human energy have taken the place of the Holy Spirit. That was true of the Galatians and the Corinthians. You remember that Paul said to them that he could not speak to them as to spiritual men because they were yet carnal. And you know how often in the course of his epistles he had to reprove and condemn them for strife and divisions.

A third thought: *What are the proofs or indications that a church like the Galatians or an individual believer is serving God in the power of the flesh—is perfecting in the flesh what was begun in the Spirit?* The answer is simple: Religious self-effort is always a manifestation of sinful flesh. What indicated the condition of the

Galatians? They were striving to be justified by the works of the law. And yet they were quarreling and in danger of devouring one another. Count up the expressions that the apostle uses to indicate their lack of love and you will find more than twelve—among them, envy, jealousy, bitterness, and strife. Read in the fourth and fifth chapters what he says about that. You will see how they tried to serve God in their own strength and utterly failed. All this religious effort resulted in failure; the power of sin and the sinful flesh got the better of them, and their whole condition was one of the saddest that could be imagined.

This comes to us with unquestionable seriousness. There is complaint everywhere in the Christian church of the lack of a high standard of integrity and godliness, even among professing believers. I remember a sermon I heard preached on business morality, and the speaker mentioned the poor conditions discovered in London. If business morality is found to be lacking, what would we find if we were to go into the homes of Christians! When we think of the life to which God has called His children and how He has promised to enable them to live by the Holy Spirit, it is hard to see the unloving attitudes and sour dispositions, sharpness of speech, bitterness, and prevalence of strife among the members of churches: envy, jealousy, sensitiveness, and pride. It compels us to ask, "Where are the signs of the presence of the Spirit of the Lamb of God?" I am afraid they are sadly lacking.

Many people speak of these fleshly traits as though they are the norm and cannot be helped. Others speak of them as sins yet have given up hope of conquering them. Many speak of these things in the church and do not see the least prospect of ever having them changed. There is no prospect until there comes a radical change, until the church of God begins to see that every sin in the believer comes from the flesh, even from the fleshly life involved in striving in self-effort to serve God. Until we learn to confess our sins, until we admit that we must see God's Spirit restored in power in His church, we will fail. Where did the church begin at Pentecost? In the Spirit. But the church of the next century fell back into the deeds of the flesh. They thought to perfect the church in their own strength.

We should not think that because the Reformation restored the great doctrine of justification by faith, the power of the Holy Spirit was then fully restored. If we believe that God is going to have mercy on His church in these last days, it will be because the doctrine and the truth about the Holy Spirit will not only be studied but sought after with a whole heart; and not only because that truth will be sought after but also because ministers and congregations will be found bowing before God in deep humility with one cry: "We have grieved God's Spirit; we have tried to be Christian churches with as little as possible of God's Spirit; we have not sought to be churches filled with the Holy Spirit. Have we faced the awful indictment that the church of Christ is powerless because of its refusal to obey God? That is an awful indictment! The church redeemed by the blood of Christ and baptized by the Holy Spirit, refusing to obey God?! And yet it is true.

And why? The common answer is "We are so weak and helpless; we try to obey, we vow to obey, but somehow we fail. You fail because you do not accept the strength God offers. God alone can work out His will in you. You cannot work it out, but His Holy Spirit can. Until the church grasps this and ceases trying by human effort to do God's will, waiting upon the Holy Spirit to come with His enabling power, it will never be what God wants her to be and what He is willing to make of her.

I come now to my last thought with a question: "What is the way to restoration?" The answer is simple. If the train has been mistakenly switched off track, there is nothing to do but to come back to the point at which it was misdirected. The Galatians had no other way of returning but to come back to where they had gone wrong, to abandon all religious effort in their own strength and from seeking anything by their own work, and to surrender themselves humbly to the Holy Spirit. And there is no other way for us as individuals. Is there within your heart this consciousness: "My life is lacking in the power of the Holy Spirit"? I come to you with God's message: You cannot conceptualize what your life would be in the power of the Holy Spirit. It is too high, too blessed, and too wonderful. Nevertheless, just as truly as the everlasting Son of God came to this world and accomplished His wonderful work, just as truly as on Calvary He died and accomplished your redemption by His precious blood, so as certainly can the Holy Spirit come into your heart with His divine power to sanctify and enable you to do God's will, filling your heart with joy and strength. But we have forgotten, we have grieved, we have dishonored the Holy Spirit, and He has not been able to do His work. But I say to you: The Father in heaven loves to fill His children with His Holy Spirit. God longs to give each of you the power of the Spirit for your daily life. The command comes to us both individually and corporately. God wants His children to arise and place their sins before Him, calling upon Him for mercy. Are we so foolish? Having begun in the Spirit, are we perfecting in the flesh what was begun in the Spirit? Let us bow in shame and confess before God how our self-effort and self-confidence have been the cause of so much failure.

I have often been asked by new believers: "Why is it that I so often fail? I did promise with my whole heart to serve God; why have I failed?" To such a question I always give the same answer: "You are trying to do in your own strength what Christ alone can do in you." And when I am asked, "I knew Christ alone could do it. I was not trusting in myself. How is it possible that I have failed?" my answer always is that they *were* trusting in themselves, otherwise they could not have failed. If they had trusted Christ, He could not fail. Perfecting in the flesh what was begun in the Spirit runs deeper than we know. God must reveal to our innermost being that it is only when we see our selfishness, sinfulness, and helplessness as He sees it that we are prepared to receive the fullness of the Spirit.

I have but *two questions*: Are you living under the power of the Holy Spirit? Are you living as an anointed, Spirit-filled person in your ministry and life before God? Remember our place is one of solemn responsibility. We are to demonstrate to others what God will do, not in our words and teaching, but in our life. God help us to do it! I remind every believer: Remember, you cannot live the Christian life on your own. You must be fully consecrated and completely surrendered to the Spirit in order for Him to work through you. Confess every failure in disposition, in speech, in attitude, every failure resulting from the absence of the Holy Spirit and the presence of self.

If your answer to the two questions is no, then I come with this one: Are you willing to be consecrated? Are you willing to surrender yourself to the power of the Holy Spirit?

You know very well, I trust, that the human side of consecration will not help you. I may consecrate myself a hundred times with all the intensity of my being, but that will not help me unless God accepts and seals the consecration.

Are you willing to surrender yourself to the Holy Spirit? You can do it now. A great deal may still be dark or dim and beyond understanding, and you may feel nothing; but come. Go into God's presence and meet God himself. God alone can effect the change. God alone, who gave us the Holy Spirit, can restore the Holy Spirit in power into your life. God alone can "strengthen us with might by his Spirit in the inner man." You who have been praying for God's blessing, look to God and say, "If you are not with us, nothing will help us." Unless God meets us, we can attend meetings for a month and only receive a little quickening and awakening. Only God can help us on a permanent basis. And God will help us if we cast ourselves in helplessness before Him. Let us ask God if He will not in His great mercy visit our souls. Let us at every meeting and every opportunity, plead with Him, "Lord, come and visit your church and let the power of the Holy Spirit be manifested among us." And with that expectation let us say, *Lord, I claim for myself and for my fellow believers the presence and the power of the Holy Spirit.* To every waiting heart that will make the sacrifice, surrender all, and take time to cry and pray to God, the answer will come. The blessing is not far off. Our God delights to help us. He will enable us to perfect in the Spirit what was begun in the Spirit.

Now, concerning the first part of this keeping, there is no question. God keeps the inheritance in heaven perfectly and safely. Yet the same God keeps *me* for the inheritance. That is what I want you to understand. You know it would be foolish for an earthly father to establish an inheritance for his children—to keep it for them—and yet not seek to keep them for it. Picture a man spending his whole lifetime making every sacrifice to amass money, and as he reaches his first million, you ask him why he sacrifices himself so much, and his answer is: "I want to leave my children a large inheritance. I am keeping it for them." If you were then to hear that the same man takes no trouble to educate his children, that he allows them to run wild in the streets and to go off in paths of sin and ignorance and folly, what would you think of him? You would say, "How foolish to keep an inheritance for his children but not keep or prepare his children for the inheritance." Yet many believers think God is keeping the inheritance for them, but they cannot believe God is keeping them for the inheritance. The same power, the same love, the same God is doing both.

I have already said that we have two very simple truths: *We are kept by the power of God* and *we are kept through faith.*

First, let's look at the divine side—*We are kept by the power of God.* Think, first of all, that *this keeping is all-inclusive.* What is kept? *You* are kept. How much of you? Your whole being. Does God keep one part of you and not another? No. Some people think in terms of a vague, general keeping; that God will keep them in such a way that when they die they will get to heaven. But they do not apply that word *kept* to everything in their being and nature. And yet that is what God wants. Imagine that I borrow a watch from a friend who says to me, "When you go to

Europe, I will let you take it with you, but keep it safe and bring it back." Now, suppose I damaged the watch: The hands were broken, the face scratched, and some of the wheels and springs destroyed. If I took it back in that condition, my friend would say, "I gave you the watch on the condition that you would keep it."

"Have I not kept it?" I say. "Here is the watch."

"But I did not mean for you to keep it only in a general way, so that you would bring back only the watch itself, even though broken. I expected you to keep every part of it, and in good order." Similarly, God does not want to keep us in this general way, so that at the last, somehow or other, we shall be saved as by fire and barely make it into heaven. Rather, the keeping power and the love of God apply to every particular of our being.

Some people think God will keep them in spiritual things but not in temporal things. This latter, they say, lies outside of His jurisdiction. But when God sends you to work in the world, He does not say, "I must leave now, while you go and earn your own livelihood." He knows you are not able to keep yourself. Rather, God says, "My child, there is no work you are to do, no business in which you are engaged, and not a penny you are to spend, but that I, your Father, will not be with you in my keeping power." God not only cares for the spiritual but for the temporal as well. The greater part of many people's lives must be spent, sometimes eight or nine or ten hours a day, amid the temptations and distractions of business; but God will care for you there. The keeping of God includes everything.

There are other people who think that in a time of trial God keeps them, but in times of prosperity they do not need His keeping; then they forget Him and let Him go. Others think the very opposite. They think that in times of prosperity, when things are smooth and quiet, they are able to cling to God, but when heavy trials come, somehow their will rebels and God cannot keep them. I tell you that in prosperity as in adversity, on good days and bad, your God is ready to keep you all the time. Yet there are others who think that God will keep them from doing some gross sin, but from small sins they cannot expect to be kept. There is, for instance, the sin of bad temper. They cannot expect God to conquer that. When you hear of someone who has gone astray or fallen into drunkenness or murder, you thank God for His keeping power. "I might have done the same as that man," you say, "if God had not kept me." And you believe He has kept you from such things. So why can't you believe that God can keep you from outbreaks of temper? You thought it was less important; you didn't remember that the great commandment of the New Testament is "Love one another as I have loved you." And when your temper and hasty judgment and sharp words came out, you sinned against the highest law—the law of God's love. Yet you say, "God will not, cannot—*does not* keep me from that." Perhaps you say, "He can"; yet deep down you feel there is something in you that keeps you from deliverance, and that God does not take it away.

Do you think believers live a holier life than is generally lived? Can believers always experience the keeping power of God with regard to sin? Can believers be kept in fellowship with God? The Word of God says we are *kept by the power of God*. There is no qualifying clause to these words. The meaning is that if you will entrust yourself entirely and absolutely to the omnipotence of God, He will delight to keep you.

Some people do not believe it possible that every word of their mouth should be to the glory of God. But it is what God desires, indeed it is what God expects from them. God is willing to place a guard at the door of their mouth, and if He will do that, can He not keep their tongue and their lips? He can; that is what God will do for those who trust Him. God's keeping is all-inclusive, and I want everyone who desires to live a holy life to think about all their weaknesses, all their shortcomings, all their sins, and to say, "Is there any sin or weakness that my God could not keep me from?" And the heart will have to answer: "No. God can keep me from all of these."

Second, if you want to understand this keeping, remember that it is not only an all-inclusive keeping but an *almighty keeping*. I want that truth burned into my soul. I want to worship God until my whole heart is filled with the thought of His omnipotence. God is almighty, and the almighty God offers himself to work in my heart, to do the work of keeping me. I want to be linked with the Omnipotent One, to the living God, and to have my place in the hollow of His hand. As you read the Psalms, think of the wonderful thoughts in many of David's expressions: for instance, when he speaks about God being *our God, our fortress, our refuge, our strong tower, our strength,* and *our salvation.* David had very wonderful visions of how the everlasting God himself is the hiding place of the believing soul, and of how He takes the believer and keeps him in the very hollow of His hand, in the secret of His pavilion, under the shadow of His wings, under His very feathers. And there David lived. Yet we who are the children of Pentecost, we who have known Christ and His sacrifice and the Holy Spirit sent down from heaven, why is it we know so little of what it is to walk step by step with the almighty God as our keeper?

Have you ever considered that in every action of grace in your heart, you have the whole omnipotence of God working to bless you? When a man gives me a gift of money, I receive it and walk away. He has given me *something* of his; the rest he keeps for himself. But that is not how it is with the power of God. God can part with nothing of His own power; therefore I can experience the power and goodness of God only to the extent that I am in contact and fellowship with Him. When I am in fellowship with Him, I am in contact also with the whole omnipotence of God and have it to help me every day. Think of a son who has a very rich father, and as the son is about to start his own business, the father says, "You can have as much money as you need to get started." All the father has is at the disposal of his son. That is the way it is with God. It is almost beyond our imagination; we feel so insignificant. His omnipotence has decided to keep someone so unworthy! His omnipotence is needed to keep every insignificant person that lives on the earth, and also to keep the universe, but how much more is it needed to keep your soul and mine from the power of sin.

If you want to grow in grace, learn to begin here: In all your musings and meditations, thoughts and deeds, studies and prayers, learn to be kept by your almighty God. What is God not going to do for the child that trusts Him? The Bible says, "Above all that we can ask or think." When you learn to know and trust Him in His power, you will live as a believer should. How little we understand that a godly life is a life full of God, a life that loves God and waits on Him, that trusts Him and allows Him to bless it! We can do the will of God only by the power of God. God gives us the first experience of His power to prepare us to desire more and to come and claim all that He can do. God help us to trust Him more every day.

This keeping is not only all-inclusive and omnipotent but also continuous and unbroken. People sometimes say, "For a week or a month God has kept me very wonderfully. I have lived in the light of His countenance and cannot tell what joy I have had in fellowship with Him. He has blessed me in my work for others. Lives have been changed, and at times I have felt as if I were carried on eagles' wings. But it did not continue. It was too good to last." Some say, "It was necessary that I should fall to keep me humble." And others: "I know it was my own fault; but somehow you cannot always live on such a level." O beloved, why is it? Can there be any reason why the keeping of God should not be continuous and unbroken? Just think. All of life is in unbroken continuity. Life is continuous, and the life of God is the life of His church and His almighty power working in us. God comes to us as the Almighty One, and without any condition He offers to be our keeper. His keeping means that day-by-day, moment-by-moment, He is going to keep us.

If I were to ask you, "Do you think God is able to keep you one whole day from actual transgression?" some of you would answer, "I not only know He is able to do it, but I think He has done it. There have been days in which He has kept my heart in His holy presence and kept me from conscious, actual transgression." Now, if He can do that for a minute or an hour or a day, why not for two days? Let us make God's omnipotence as revealed in His Word the measure of our expectations. Has God not said in His Word, "I, the Lord, do keep it, and will water it, every moment"? What can that mean? Does "every moment" mean every moment? Did God promise of that vineyard of red wine that *every moment* He would water it so that the heat of the sun and the scorching wind might never dry it up? Yes. In South Africa when they graft branches together, they sometimes tie a bottle of water above it so that now and then a drop of water will saturate what they have joined together. The moisture is kept there unceasingly until the graft has had time to fully join together and resist the heat of the sun. Will our God, in His tenderhearted love toward us, not keep us every moment when He has promised to do so? If we could only see that our whole life is to be God's doing: "It is God who works in us to will and to do of His good pleasure." When we finally exercise faith to expect this from God, God will do all for us.

The keeping is to be continuous. Every morning God will meet you as you awaken. There is no question about it. If you trust God, He will meet you every morning with His divine sunshine and love. He will give you the confidence: "Today I have God to keep me continuously by His almighty power." And God will meet you the next day and every day; never mind if in the practice of fellowship there comes occasional failure. If you maintain your position and say, *Lord, I am going to expect you to do your utmost, and I am going to trust you day by day to keep me absolutely,* your faith will grow stronger and stronger and you will know the unbroken keeping power of God.

Now, for the other side—*We are kept by the power of God through faith.* How should we understand this faith? Let me say, first of all, that this faith means utter powerlessness and helplessness before God. At the bottom of all faith there is a feeling of helplessness. If I am in the process of buying a house, I entrust a Realtor with the work of getting the transfer of the property into my name and making all the legal arrangements. I cannot do that work, and in trusting my Realtor, I confess I cannot do it. Similarly, faith always means helplessness. Sometimes it means: I can do it with a great deal of trouble, but another can do it better. But in most cases it is utter helplessness; *another must do it for me.* And that is the secret of the spiritual life. A man must learn to say, "I surrender everything; I have tried and desired, thought and prayed, but have failed. God has blessed and helped me, but still, in the long run, there has been so much of sin and sadness." What a change comes when a man is broken down into utter helplessness and self-despair and says, "I can do nothing!"

Remember Paul. He was living a blessed life, had been taken up into the third heaven, and then the thorn in the flesh came, "a messenger of Satan to buffet him." And what happened? Paul could not understand it, so he prayed that the Lord would take it away; but the Lord said, in effect, "No, there is the danger of your exalting yourself. Therefore, I have sent you this trial to keep you humble before me." Paul then learned a lesson that he would never forgot—to rejoice in his infirmities. He said that the weaker he was the better it was for him, for when he was weak he was strong in his Lord.

Do you want to enter what people call "the higher life"? Then go a step lower. I remember being told about someone who visited a factory to observe a new technological system. To view the operation, the man's friend wanted to take him up to the top of the tower to see how the work was done. The man came to the tower, entered by the door, and began going upstairs, but his friend said, "No. That's the wrong way. We must go downstairs first." The gentleman took him down a long set of stairs, and there an elevator was waiting to take them to the top. He said, "There's a lesson in this: going down is often the best way to get to the top." Yes, God will have to bring us down very low; we will have to come to a place of emptiness and despair and nothingness. It is when we sink down in utter helplessness that the everlasting God will reveal himself in His power and that our hearts will learn to trust God alone.

What is it that keeps us from trusting Him perfectly? Many say, "I believe what you say, but there is one difficulty. If my trust were perfect, all would be right, for I know God will honor trust. But how am I to get that trust?" Through the death of self. The great hindrance to trust is self-effort. As long as you have your own wisdom and thoughts and strength, you cannot fully trust God. But when God breaks you down, when everything begins to grow dim before your eyes and you see that you understand nothing, then God is near. If you will wait upon God, He will become all you need. *As long as we are something, God cannot be all,* and His omnipotence cannot do its full work. That is the beginning of faith—utter despair of self and dependence on God alone.

Next we must understand that *faith is rest.* In the beginning of the faith-life, faith is struggling; but as long as faith is struggling, it has not attained its full strength. But when faith's struggles come to an end, and we cast our self upon God and rest in Him, then joy and victory come.

In my introduction, I mentioned how the Keswick Convention began. I told you about Canon Battersby and his search for victory over sin. When he heard about the possibility of victory, he truly desired it, but it was as if he could not reach it. On one occasion, he heard a message on rest and faith from the story of the nobleman who came from Capernaum to Cana to ask Christ to heal his child. In the message it was shown that the nobleman believed that Christ could help him in a general way, but he really came to Jesus by way of an experiment. He hoped Christ would help him, but he was not convinced of that help. But when Christ said to him, "Go your way, for your child lives," that man believed the word Jesus spoke; in fact, he rested in it. He had no proof that his child was well, and he had a return walk of seven hours' journey to Capernaum. On his way back, he met his servant, who brought the first news that the child was well. At one o'clock on the afternoon of the previous day, at the very time that Jesus had spoken to him, the fever had left the child. That father rested upon the word of Jesus and His work, and he went down to Capernaum and found his child well; he praised God and became with his whole house a believer and a disciple of Jesus. That, my friends, is faith! When God comes to me with the promise of His keeping, and I have nothing on earth to trust in, I say to God, "Your word is enough"; "kept by the power of God." That is faith and that is rest.

After Canon Battersby heard that message, he went home and in the darkness of the night found rest. He rested on the word of Jesus. The next morning, in the streets of Oxford, he said to a friend, "I have found it!" Then he went and told others and the Keswick Convention was started so that those at the convention, along with himself, should testify simply to what God had done.

It is a great thing when a man comes to rest on God's almighty power for every moment of his life with regard to temptations to haste, anger, unloving attitudes, pride, and sin in general. It is a great thing to enter into a covenant with the omnipotent Jehovah, not because of anything that any man says or his heart feels, but on the strength of the Word of God: "Kept by the power of God through faith." Let us say to God that we are going to prove Him to the very uttermost. Let us say, "We ask you for nothing more than you can give, but we want nothing less." Say also, "Let my life be a proof of what the omnipotent God can do." Let these be the two dispositions of our souls every day—deep helplessness and simple, childlike rest.

One more thought in regard to faith: *Faith implies fellowship with God.* Many people want to take the Word and believe it, but they find they cannot. You cannot separate God from His Word. No goodness or power can be received apart from God; and if you want to get into this life of godliness, you *must* take time for fellowship with God.

People sometimes tell me, "My life is so hurried and busy that I have no time for fellowship with God." A dear missionary said to me, "People do not know how we missionaries are tempted. I get up at five o'clock in the morning and there are the nationals waiting for their orders for work. Then I have to go to school and spend hours there; and then there is other work. Sixteen hours rush along, and I hardly get time to be alone with God." There is the problem. I want you to remember two things. I have not told you to trust the omnipotence of God as a mere object, and I have not told you to trust the Word of God as a mere book, but I have told you to go to the God of omnipotence and the God of the Word. Deal with God as that nobleman dealt with the living Christ. Why was he able to believe the word that Christ spoke to him? Because in the very eyes and tones and voice of Jesus, the Son of God, he saw and heard something that caused him to feel that he could trust Him. And that is what Christ can do for you and me. Do not try to stir up faith from within. How often I have tried to do that and made a fool of myself! You cannot stir up faith from the depths of your heart. Leave your heart and look into the face of Christ and listen to what He tells you about how He will keep you. Look up into the face of your loving Father. Take time every day with Him and begin a new life with the deep emptiness and poverty of a man who has nothing and who waits to receive everything from Him; with the deep restfulness of a man who rests on the living God, the omnipotent Jehovah; and prove Him if He will not open the windows of heaven and pour out a blessing too large to contain.

I close by asking you if you are willing to fully experience the heavenly keeping for the heavenly inheritance. Robert Murray M'Cheyne said, "O God, make me as holy as a pardoned sinner can be made." And if you will say that earnestly, from the depths of your heart, come and enter into a covenant with the everlasting and omnipotent Jehovah, and in great helplessness, but in great restfulness, place yourself into His hands. And then as you enter into your covenant, take with you the promise that the everlasting God is going to be your companion, holding your hand every moment. Our keeper is watching over us without a moment's interval; our Father is delighting to reveal himself to our souls. He has the power to let the sunshine of His love shine on us all day. Do not be afraid that because you have a secular job, you cannot have God with you always. Learn a lesson from the natural sun that shines upon you all day; wherever you are, God takes care that it shines upon you. And God will see that His own divine light shines upon you and that you abide in that light. Let us trust God to do it.

Listen to these last words. Here is the omnipotence of God, and here is faith reaching out to the measure of that omnipotence. Can we say, "I am going to trust my God for all His omnipotence can do"? Are not the two sides of this heavenly life wonderful? God's omnipotence covering me, and my will in its smallness resting in that omnipotence and rejoicing in it!

Chapter 14

You Are the Branches

In this final chapter, my desire is to speak especially to those in Christian work. The primary thought in my heart in this regard is that everything depends on our being in a right relationship with Jesus Christ. If I want good apples, I must have a good apple tree; and if I care for the health of the apple tree, the apple tree will give me good apples. The same is true in our Christian work. *If our life with Christ is right,* all will come out right in the ministry. There may be a need for instruction, help, and training in the various areas of the work, and all of that has its proper place. But in the long run, the first requirement is to have our life in Christ; in other words, to have Christ in us, working through us. I pray that God may comfort and encourage every beloved servant of His. I know how in the ministry there is much that can disturb us or cause anxious questions; but the Master desires that we be at peace and rest in our service for Him, that we have joy and strength to carry out our work. But this is only possible if we abide in Him and maintain the right attitude.

I have taken my thoughts from the parable of the vine and the branches in John 15:5: "I am the vine; you are the branches." I want to consider especially the words *you are the branches.*

It is really a simple thing to be a branch of a tree or a vine. The branch grows out of the vine or the tree, and there it lives and grows and, in due time, bears fruit. It has no responsibility except to receive from the root and stem its nourishment through the sap. Similarly, if by the Holy Spirit we understood our relationship to Jesus Christ, our work would be transformed into a most effectual influence. Instead of being an exhausting experience, our work could be new and fresh, linking us to Jesus as never before. After all, isn't it true that our work often comes *between* Jesus and us? What madness! The very work we do for Him can be taken up in such a way that it separates us from Christ. Many laborers in the "vineyard" have complained that they have too much work to do and not enough time for close communion with Jesus; in fact, some work decreases the inclination for prayer, and intense involvement with needy people darkens the spiritual life! What a tragedy, that the bearing of fruit should separate the branch from the vine! Surely this is because we have looked upon our work as something *other than* bearing fruit. May God deliver us from every false thought or expectation about the Christian life.

Here are a few thoughts about what should be the blessed branch-life.

First, it is *a life of absolute dependence*. The branch has nothing of itself; it depends upon the vine for everything. The phrase "absolute dependence" is quite significant. A great German theologian wrote two large volumes some years ago to show that the whole of Calvin's theology is summed up in the one principle of *absolute dependence upon God*. Another great writer has said that *absolute, unalterable dependence upon God alone* is the essence of the religion of angels, and should be that of men also. God is everything to the angels and is willing to be everything to the believer. If we can learn every moment of the day to depend upon God, everything will come out as it should. You will receive the "higher" life if you depend absolutely upon God.

The relationship between a vine and its branches is one of interdependence. Every vine you see and every cluster of grapes that appears on your table is a reminder of that relationship. The branch is absolutely dependent on the vine for its fruit. The vine counts on the branch to bear the fruit.

Of course, the vine has the vital work to do. It sends its roots down into the soil, under the ground—the roots often far-reaching—and finds nourishment and moisture. If fertilizer is added to the soil, the vine sends its roots toward it; then the roots turn the moisture and fertilizer into a special sap that energizes the growth of the rich fruit to be borne. The vine does the work; the branch simply receives from the vine the sap to grow the grapes. I have been told of a particular vine that sometimes bore a couple of thousand clusters of grapes. People were astonished at its unusual production. Afterward it was discovered the vine stretched its roots hundreds of yards underground to the River Thames. There, in all the rich soil of the riverbed, it had found abundant nourishment and moisture, and the roots drew the sap that incredible distance into the vine, resulting in an astounding harvest.

Jesus is the Vine. The power of the Holy Spirit works in us, the branches, to produce wonderful fruit for the kingdom as we abide in Him. Whether I preach a sermon, teach a Bible class, or visit the sick of my congregation, all the responsibility of the work is on God, who supplies the strength.

The flow of power to the branches is not intermittent. It is a vital relationship that is ongoing and healthy. The branch abiding in the vine is our position as a servant. Every day I must be conscious of my part to abide in Him, to rest and trust and know that without the Vine I am nothing. Study the word *nothing*. If I am something, God cannot be everything. We need to become nothing.

This is our first lesson, that of learning to be absolutely dependent. Dependence upon God is the secret of all power in our work. The branch has nothing except what it receives from the vine, and you and I have nothing except what we receive from Jesus.

Second, besides being entirely dependent, a branch is *at rest*. If it could think and speak, the branch would teach us the importance of resting in our Lord Jesus. It would say, "With all your hurry and effort in Christ's work you never prosper. The first thing you need to do is come and rest. That is what I do: simply rest in the vine. When spring comes, I have no anxious thought or care. The vine pours its sap into me to give to the bud and the leaf. When summer comes, I have no care; in the great heat I trust the vine to bring moisture to keep me fresh. In the time of harvest, when the owner comes to pluck the grapes, I have no care. If something is not good about the grapes, the owner never blames the branch; the blame rests with the vine. And if you would be a true branch of Christ, the living Vine, just rest in Him. Let Christ bear the responsibility."

You may say, "Won't that make me lazy?" No one who learns to rest in the living Christ can become lazy, for the closer your contact with Christ, the more of the Spirit of His zeal and love will be borne in you. Begin to work into the midst of your entire dependence the addition of *deep restfulness*. A man sometimes tries with great effort to be dependent upon Christ, but he stresses himself about this absolute dependence; he struggles, and he cannot quite get it. But let him only sit back, sink down, rest his entire weight on Christ every day.

> In Thy strong hand I lay me down,
> So shall the work be done;
> For who can work so wondrously
> As the Almighty One?

Servant of God, take your place every day at the feet of Jesus, in the blessed peace and rest that come from the knowledge:

> I have no care,
> my cares are His;
> I have no fear,
> He cares for all my fears.

Come, children of God, and understand that it is the Lord Jesus who wants to work through you. You complain of your lack of fervent love. It will come from Jesus. He will pour divine love into your heart so that you can love people. That is the meaning of the assurance "The love of God is shed abroad in our hearts by the Holy Spirit"; and of the other word, "The love of Christ constrains us." Christ can put in you such a fountain of love that you cannot help but love the most wretched, the most ungrateful, even those who have tried you the most. Rest in Christ, who gives wisdom and strength. You do not realize how restfulness will often prove to be the best part of your witness. If you plead and argue with people, they will only understand that you are striving with them. It will only be as if two men are not in agreement and are struggling on an earthly level with each other. But if you will let the deep rest of God envelop you, the peace and quiet and holiness of heaven will open the heart of the listener to hear the words you speak.

Third, *the branch teaches a lesson of fruitfulness.* The Lord Jesus repeated the word *fruit* often in this parable. He spoke first of *fruit,* then of *more fruit,* and then of *much fruit.* You are ordained not only to bear fruit, but to bear *much fruit.* "In this is my Father glorified, *that you bear much fruit.*" In the first place, Christ said, "I am the Vine, and my Father is the Vinedresser." My Father is the Vinedresser, who has charge of you and me. He who will watch over the connection between Christ and the branches is God; and it is in the power of God through Christ that we are to bear fruit.

We know the world is perishing for lack of laborers. But many in the work of the harvest are saying, "We need not only more workers, but our workers need to have new power, a life that produces fruit." Child of God, I appeal to you. Think of the trouble you take, in the case of a sick friend or family member, to find a cure for his pain or sickness. You will go to any length to provide the help he needs. Yet all around us are hundreds who never go to church or who may attend services but do not know Christ. Salvation is in the fruit of the Vine. It is a matter of offering the grapes of the Heavenly Vine. These are not available to buy, as we know. Unless the children of God are filled with the Holy Spirit and the love of Jesus, they cannot offer the life-giving grape. We all confess there is a great deal of work going on, a great deal of preaching and teaching and visiting, a great deal of earnest effort, but there is very little manifestation of the power of God.

What is the problem? There is a faulty connection between the branch and the Vine. Christ, the Heavenly Vine, has blessings to pour out on tens of thousands who are perishing. Christ, the

Heavenly Vine, has power to provide the heavenly grapes. But we are the branches, and we cannot bear heavenly fruit unless we are in vital relationship with Jesus Christ.

Do not confuse work and fruit. There may be a good deal of work for Christ that is not the fruit of the Heavenly Vine. Do not seek only to be busy for God. Study to know what is true fruit-bearing. It is the very life, power, Spirit, and love from the heart of the Son of God expressing itself through you to the world.

You are aware of the fact that there are many different kinds of grapes. From country to country there comes a great variety, each bearing a different name. And every vine provides exactly that peculiar aroma and juice that gives the grape its particular texture and taste. Christ, our Vine, has a life full of love, blessing, and power for all who trust in Him that is entirely heavenly and divine, and that will enter our hearts and make us like Him. Remain in close connection with the Heavenly Vine and pray, *Lord Jesus, nothing less than the life-giving sap that flows through yourself, nothing less than the Spirit of your divine life is what I ask for. May your Holy Spirit flow through me in all my work for you.* I remind you that the sap of the Heavenly Vine is the Holy Spirit himself. The Holy Spirit is the life of the Heavenly Vine. What you must receive from Christ is nothing less than a strong inflowing of the Holy Spirit. You need it desperately, but you need nothing more than that. Do not expect Christ to give only a bit of strength here and a bit of blessing there. As the vine does its work in providing its own peculiar sap to the branch, so expect Christ to give His own Holy Spirit into your heart, and then you will bear much fruit. If you have only begun to bear fruit and are listening to the word of Christ in the parable referring to "more fruit" and "much fruit," remember that in order to bear more fruit you simply need more of Jesus in your life and heart.

We ministers of the Gospel are in danger of getting into a pattern of undaunted *work*! We may pray about it, but the freshness and buoyancy and joy of the heavenly life are not always present. Let us seek to understand that the life of the branch is a life of much fruit because it is a life rooted in Christ, the living, Heavenly Vine.

The fourth thought addresses the truth that *the life of the branch is a life of close communion.* Let us ask again: What does the branch have to do? You know that precious inexhaustible word that Christ used: *abide.* Your life is to be an abiding life. And what is abiding like? It is as simple as the relationship of a branch to a vine: close fellowship every moment of the day. Can we not live every day in abiding communion with the Heavenly Vine? Many would respond, "But I am so occupied with other things." Even if you have ten hours of work every day in which you are occupied with temporal things, it should not hinder your abiding in Christ; abiding is a work of the *heart,* not of a physical location or even a conscious effort. It is a knowing, loving, confident relationship deep down in the inner life characterized by faith and hope and spontaneous communication. If you will learn to draw on this relationship at any time and be led by the Spirit on a moment-by-moment basis, you will find that fruit will come.

How is my life affected by this abiding communion? What does it mean? I will be consulting my Lord about every major decision, even minor ones. I will spend time in private prayer. Some will occasionally receive a great blessing, sense a great inflow of heavenly joy, but this will not necessarily be the norm. A lack of excitement does not mean our communion is broken. Yes, we will take time to be alone with Christ, but His presence will not leave us even if we are not conscious of it.

Many believers look upon this abiding as a burden, a duty, and a difficulty! This is very unfortunate. It is a great hindrance to progress in the Christian life. We need more quiet fellowship with God, but never think of it as a duty. It is our joy and our privilege. You cannot be a healthy branch without communion with God. But let it come naturally as a friend-to-friend conversation would be. Jesus longs to live in close communion with you. May it be your heart's desire too.

My last thought is that *the life of the branch is a life of entire surrender.* It is a surrender that is complete, absolute, without reservation. This kind of commitment leaves all responsibility to the vine to give as much or as little sap as it chooses. We are at its disposal, and the vine can do with us what it likes.

The more I minister, the more I feel that absolute surrender is one of the most difficult points to make clear and yet one of the most important of our Christian lives. Often it is easy for a person to come and offer himself to God for entire consecration without knowing exactly what is meant by it. Our surrender to Christ should be as complete as Christ's surrender to God when He walked on the earth. Some think that is too radical. But that is what is needed. Christ Jesus came to breathe His own Spirit into us, to make us find our very highest happiness in living entirely for God, just as He did. I would live day by day that Christ might be able to do with me what He desires.

A terrible mistake lies at the bottom of so much effort to follow Christ. A man thinks: *I have my business, my family duties, and my civic responsibility, and all this will not change. Now besides all this, I hope to serve God and be kept from sin and made fit for heaven. God help me to perform my duties.* But this is not as it should be. When Christ died, He bought the sinner with His blood. Our relationship as a Christian is one of servant to master. If I have been bought with the blood of Christ, and I choose to follow Him, I must live every day with the one thought: *How can I please my Master?* Other relationships in life are secondary to this one.

We find the Christian life so difficult because we seek for God's blessing while we live the Christian life according to our own wishes and whims. We make our own plans and choose our own work, and then we ask the Lord Jesus to bless us. But our relationship to Jesus should be such that we are entirely at His disposal, coming to Him every day humbly and honestly, saying, "Lord, is there anything in me that is not according to your will, that has not been ordered by you, or that is not entirely surrendered to you?" If we would wait patiently, I know what the result would be. There would spring up a relationship between Christ and us so close and so tender that we would be amazed at how we could have thought we were surrendered to Christ.

When I speak of full surrender, I am not speaking about the surrender of our sins, though it may be that you need to do that: perhaps a violent temper, a bad habit, sins that have never been given up for the sake of your relationship with Christ. I am afraid that unconsciously many compromise, having the idea that they cannot be without sin; that we all must sin every day; we cannot help it. But our cry to God should be: "Lord, keep me from sin!" Surrender is about yielding yourself completely to Jesus. He will speak to you about any sin that you are not aware of.

There is so much worldliness in our work, in our churches, and in our surroundings that we have grown used to it and we think: *It cannot be changed.* We do not go to the Lord and ask

Him about it. But my advice is that you *bring everything to Jesus* and say, "Lord, everything in my life has to be in complete harmony with you." Let your surrender to Christ be absolute. He will show you what is not according to His mind and will and lead you into deeper fellowship.

In conclusion, let me say in a word, Christ Jesus is the Vine and you are the branches. If there is still in your heart the thought that you are not a strong, healthy, fruit-bearing branch, that you are not closely linked with Jesus, listen to His words: "I am the Vine; I will receive you; I will draw you to myself; I will bless you; I will strengthen you; I will fill you with My Spirit. You are the branch. I have given myself utterly to you; give yourself utterly to me. I have surrendered myself as God absolutely to you. I became Man and died for you that I might be entirely yours. Come and surrender yourself entirely to be mine."

What is your answer? Let it be a prayer from the depths of your heart that the living Christ may gather you to himself. Let your prayer be that He, the Living Vine, shall link you so closely to himself that your heart will sing: He is my Vine, and I am His branch—I want nothing more—now I have the Everlasting Vine. Then, when you are alone with Him, worship and adore Him, praise and trust Him, love Him and wait for His love: It is enough, my soul is satisfied. Glory be to His blessed name!

Jesus, the Ultimate Example

"If Jesus is to be our example—in his lowliness—we need to understand the principles in which His humility was rooted," says Andrew Murray. In twelve brief but powerful chapters he takes readers on a journey through Scripture and Christ's life, showing us the utmost need for humility—as opposed to pride—in the Christian life.

This book goes beyond merely a call for humility and illustrates for readers what humility looks like in daily life. Demonstrating for us what Christ did when he took the form of a servant, Murray calls humility a distinguishing characteristic of the believer and shows us how to embrace this attitude in our own lives.

Classic Andrew Murray edited for today's reader

Humility by Andrew Murray

BETHANYHOUSE